The fight against money laundering and terrorist financing is a pillar of U.S. national security and a strong financial system. It is an undertaking that requires the coordinated and dedicated efforts of policy makers, law enforcement, supervisors, and the private sector, particularly financial institutions. It is essential that we work closely together to develop and effectively implement strong laws and regulations to detect, deter, and disrupt illicit finance. Equally important is that we understand and communicate the money laundering and terrorist financing threats, vulnerabilities, and risks facing our country.

In this spirit, the Department of the Treasury is proud to publish the National Money Laundering Risk Assessment and National Terrorist Financing Risk Assessment. These reports – based on an analysis of more than 5,000 law enforcement cases, financial reporting by U.S. financial institutions and reports from across government and the private sector – represent an unprecedented review of the key money laundering and terrorist financing risks to the United States. The purpose of these assessments is to help the public and private sectors understand the money laundering and terrorist financing methods used in the United States, the risks that these activities pose to our financial system and national security, and the effectiveness of our current efforts to combat these methods. Our goal is to more effectively target and prevent these activities.

These assessments should be used by industry and other stakeholders to help inform a risk-based approach to identify, assess, and manage risks in compliance with their obligations under the Bank Secrecy Act and sanctions laws. It is the view of the Treasury Department that financial institutions that establish and maintain appropriate risk-based anti-money laundering programs will be well positioned to effectively manage accounts, prevent illicit transactions, and avoid enforcement action. The assessments published today should be used as one additional tool in evaluating risk, but should not be read in isolation. Additionally, these assessments can help financial institutions determine how best to efficiently allocate resources to combat money laundering and terrorist financing.

The United States has a large, complex, and open financial system – making it a destination for legitimate trade and investment, but also a target for illicit activity and actors. Our anti-money laundering and countering the financing of terrorism framework is sophisticated and well-designed to address these threats, while maintaining an attractive business environment. Our law enforcement and supervisory authorities are well equipped to investigate and take enforcement actions when our financial system is abused by illicit actors. In addition, the U.S. financial sector is a key partner in our efforts to combat illicit finance – our financial institutions devote considerable time and resources to identifying and assessing risks and in taking steps to mitigate those risks.

DEPARTMENT OF THE TREASURY
WASHINGTON, D.C.

UNDER SECRETARY

We hope these reports will be a centerpiece of the robust public and private sector efforts that are underway to mitigate the illicit finance risks facing the United States as we work together to make the U.S. financial sector the safest and most secure in the world.

Adam J. Szubin
Acting Under Secretary, Terrorism and Financial Intelligence

TABLE OF CONTENTS

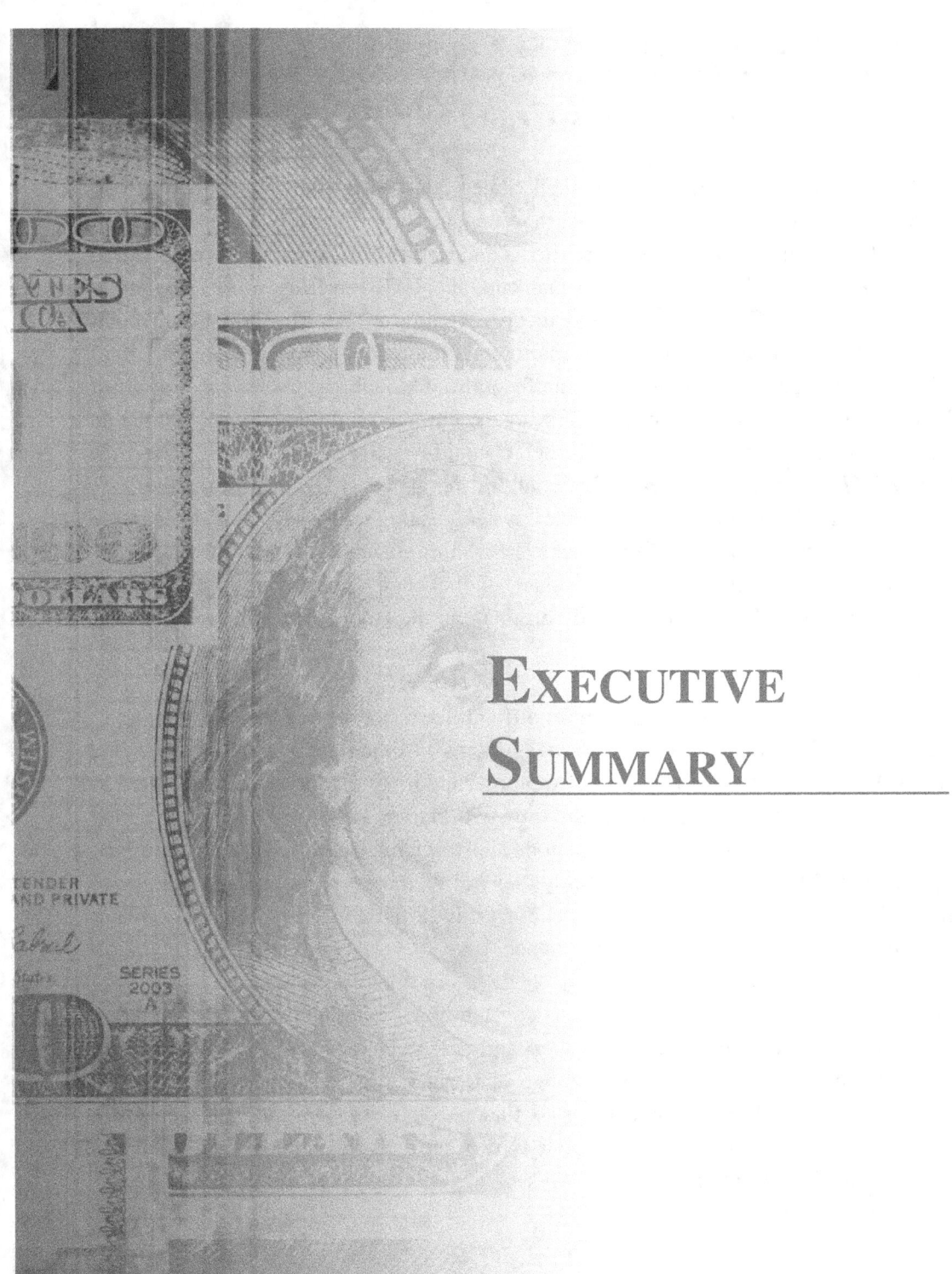

EXECUTIVE SUMMARY

1

EXECUTIVE SUMMARY

After the September 11, 2001 terrorist attacks, the United States adopted a preventive approach to combating all forms of terrorist activity. Efforts to combat the financing of terrorism (CFT) are a central pillar of this approach.[1] Cutting off financial support to terrorists and terrorist organizations is essential to disrupting their operations and preventing attacks. To that end, the U.S. government has sought to identify and disrupt ongoing terrorist financing (TF) and to prevent future TF. The law enforcement community, including various components of the U.S. Departments of Justice, Homeland Security, and the Treasury, along with the intelligence community and the federal functional regulators, applies robust authorities to identify, investigate, and combat specific TF threats, enforce compliance with applicable laws and regulations, and prosecute supporters in order to deter would-be terrorist financiers. The U.S. Department of the Treasury (Treasury), which leads financial and regulatory CFT efforts for the U.S. government, employs targeted financial sanctions, formulates systemic safeguards, and seeks to increase financial transparency to make accessing the U.S. financial system more difficult and risky for terrorists and their facilitators. All of these efforts involve extensive international engagement to try to prevent any form of TF, particularly financing that does not necessarily originate in the United States, from accessing the U.S. financial system.

These efforts have succeeded in making it significantly more difficult for terrorists and their facilitators to access and abuse the regulated U.S. and international financial systems. At the time of the September 11, 2001 attacks, Al-Qaida (AQ) was relying on both a web of wealthy supporters that practically operated in the open and a financial system that let money for terrorists flow with minimal scrutiny.[2] Operating such a financial network would be substantially more difficult today in the United States because of robust anti-money laundering (AML)/CFT standards. Additionally, several of the most significant sources of TF—such as the ability of terrorists to derive financial benefit through the control of territory—result from weak governance that the United States does not experience.

However, the threat from terrorism and terrorist financing is constantly evolving and requires adaptation by law enforcement, financial regulators, intelligence services, and policy makers. When examined over time, several fundamental lessons emerge: first, a wide range of terrorist organizations have sought to draw upon the wealth and resources of the United States to finance their organizations and activities; second, just as there is no one type of terrorist, there is no one type of terrorist financier or facilitator; and third, terrorist financiers and facilitators are creative and will seek to exploit vulnerabilities in our society and financial system to further their unlawful aims.[3]

Thus, even with the safeguards described above, the U.S. financial system continues to face residual TF risk. The central role of the U.S. financial system within the international financial system and the sheer

---

[1] *See* White House, *National Strategy for Counterterrorism*, June 2011. Available at http://www.whitehouse.gov/sites/default/files/counterterrorism_strategy.pdf.

[2] *See* National Commission on Terrorist Attacks upon the United States, Kean, T. H., & Hamilton, L. (2004). *The 9/11 Commission report: Final report of the National Commission on Terrorist Attacks upon the United States*, p.169. Washington, D.C.: National Commission on Terrorist Attacks upon the United States.

[3] *See* Michael Taxay, United States Attorneys' Bulletin, Vol. 62, No.5 (September 2014), "Terrorist Financing: Trends in the Prosecution of Terrorist Financing and Facilitation." Available at http://www.justice.gov/usao/eousa/foia_reading_room/usab6205.pdf.

volume and diversity of international financial transactions that in some way pass through U.S. financial institutions expose the U.S. financial system to TF risks that other financial systems may not face. As Treasury Secretary Jacob Lew has observed, "The dollar is the world's reserve currency and, for over 200 years, we have established ourselves as the backbone of the global financial system."[4] While U.S. counterterrorism (CT)/CFT efforts have resulted in better identification and faster action than prior to September 11, 2001, information obtained from financial institution reporting, TF-related prosecutions, and enforcement actions against financial institutions in the United States are powerful reminders of the TF risk that remains in the United States.

As described in detail in Section III, multiple terrorist organizations and radicalized individuals seek to exploit several vulnerabilities in the United States and in the U.S. financial system to raise and move funds, that despite ongoing efforts by the U.S. government to mitigate, still pose a residual risk of TF. Terrorist financiers use various criminal schemes to raise funds in the United States, and they continue to attempt to exploit the generosity of American citizens. Although coordinated law enforcement and regulatory efforts by the U.S. government, working with charitable organizations, has improved the resiliency of the charitable sector to abuse by TF facilitators, the large size and diversity of the U.S. charitable sector and its global reach means the sector remains vulnerable to abuse. A notable trend identified in the charitable sector involves individuals supporting various terrorist groups seeking to raise funds in the United States under the auspices of charitable giving, but outside of any charitable organization recognized by the U.S. government. Additionally, the growth of online communication networks, including social media, has opened up new avenues for terrorists and their supporters to solicit directly, and receive funds from, U.S. residents.

In terms of moving and placing funds, while the United States has reduced the ability of terrorist groups to use regulated financial institutions to move funds through the U.S. financial system through effective regulation, supervision, investigations and enforcement, some residual risks remain, due to correspondent banking relationships with foreign financial institutions and the acts of complicit money services business (MSB) employees in the United States. Unlicensed money transmitters may also be used to send funds abroad, and there are aggressive investigation, prosecution, and regulatory efforts underway to detect and disrupt such activity.

Because other more effective funds transmission routes are disrupted, the use of cash smuggling to move funds across U.S. borders — while slower, less efficient, and more expensive than regulated or unregulated financial institutions — continues to be employed by a variety of terrorist groups.

The U.S. government is also closely monitoring several emerging TF threats and vulnerabilities, including the use of cybercrime and identity theft schemes by terrorist groups and individuals to raise funds, as well as the use of new payment systems to move and place funds.

---

[4] Jacob J. Lew, Secretary of the Treasury, "Lessons From a Crisis," New York Times, October 20, 2013.

INTRODUCTION

INTRODUCTION

The National Terrorist Financing (TF) Risk Assessment identifies the TF risks that are of priority concern to the United States. The purpose of the National TF Risk Assessment is to identify and understand the TF threats and vulnerabilities in the United States, assess current efforts to combat these threats and vulnerabilities, and understand the remaining risk to the U.S. financial system and national security.

The National TF Risk Assessment complements the 2015 National Money Laundering (ML) Risk Assessment in order to provide a similar depiction of the threat posed by TF. In particular, the assessment:

- Examines methods used in TF-related federal prosecutions;

- Draws from the work of the interagency Working Group on Combating Terrorist Financing, led by Treasury, which assesses threats, trends, and risks in the United States; and

- Identifies priority residual TF risks.

PARTICIPANTS

The National TF Risk Assessment was drafted by Treasury's Office of Terrorist Financing and Financial Crimes (TFFC). In preparing the National TF Risk Assessment, TFFC consulted with the following offices and agencies:

- Department of the Treasury
  - Terrorism and Financing Intelligence (TFI)
    - Financial Crimes Enforcement Network (FinCEN)
    - Office of Foreign Assets Control (OFAC)
    - Office of Intelligence and Analysis (OIA)
    - Treasury Executive Office of Asset Forfeiture (TEOAF)
  - Internal Revenue Service (IRS)
    - Criminal Investigation (CI)
    - Tax Exempt & Government Entities Division (TE/GE)
    - Small Business/Self Employed Division (SB/SE)
- Department of Justice (DOJ)
  - National Security Division (NSD)
  - Tax Division
  - Drug Enforcement Administration (DEA)
  - Federal Bureau of Investigation-Terrorist Financing Operations Section (FBI-TFOS)
- Department of Homeland Security (DHS)

- o Immigration and Customs Enforcement (ICE), Homeland Security Investigations (HSI)
- o Customs and Border Protection (CBP)
- o Office of Intelligence and Analysis
- Department of State (DOS)
  - o Bureau of Counterterrorism
  - o Bureau of Economic and Business Affairs
  - o Bureau of International Narcotics and Law Enforcement
- National Counterterrorism Center (NCTC)
- Staff of the Federal functional regulators (FFR)[5]

SOURCES

The National TF Risk Assessment is compiled from agency-specific, interagency, and Congressional advisories; analysis, guidance, reports, speeches, and testimony published since 2001; new domestic research and analysis; and relevant international studies. A significant number of the findings that produced the National TF Risk Assessment were informed by intelligence reporting and analysis. Although these reports cannot be made public, the risk assessment has endeavored to capture strategic, declassified aspects in order to provide a comprehensive assessment.

Public sector reports published since 2006, and referenced in footnotes throughout the National TF Risk Assessment, include:

- Agency-specific reports:
  - o United States Attorney's Bulletin
- Interagency studies and strategies:
  - o Country Reports on Terrorism
  - o 2011 National Strategy for Counterterrorism
- Congressional reports & testimony:
  - o Annual Congressional Threat Briefings by Departments of Justice and Homeland Security, Office of the Director of National Intelligence, and National Counterterrorism Center
  - o 2014 Terrorist Assets Report

---

[5] This includes staff of: the Commodity Futures Trading Commission (CFTC); Board of Governors of the Federal Reserve System (FRB); Federal Deposit Insurance Corporation (FDIC); National Credit Union Administration (NCUA); Office of the Comptroller of the Currency (OCC); and the Securities and Exchange Commission (SEC).

An analysis was conducted by the Department of the Treasury on terrorism and terrorism-related convictions between 2001 and 2014. Cases were flagged in which the defendant was charged with one or more of the below offenses:

- Title 18 of the U.S. Code, Section 2339A, which prohibits the provision of material support or resources knowing or intending that they are to be used in committing certain predicate violations associated with terrorism. Material support has been broadly defined to be any property, tangible or intangible, or service, and is not limited to physical transfers of assets (e.g. via a loan or something of value).

- Title 18 of the U.S. Code, Section 2339B, which prohibits knowingly providing material support or resources to an entity designated by the Secretary of State as a "foreign terrorist organization" (FTO), which currently includes 59 groups.[6]

- Title 18 of the U.S. Code, Section 2339C, which prohibits the unlawful and willful provision or collection of funds with the intention or knowledge they are to be used to carry out a terrorist attack.

- Title 18 of the U.S. Code, Section 2339D, which prohibits persons from receiving military-type training from, or on behalf of, an FTO. Under an aiding or abetting theory, anyone who finances another in receiving such training would be liable as a principal.

- Title 21 of the U.S. Code, Section 960a, which prohibits persons who have engaged in certain drug offenses from knowingly providing anything of pecuniary value to terrorists.

- Title 50 of the U.S. Code, Section 1705, which prohibits engaging in financial interactions with a person or entity that has been named as a Specially Designated Global Terrorist (SDGT), unless OFAC has issued a license permitting the transaction. This also prohibits making or receiving any contribution of funds, goods, or services to or for the benefit of an SDGT.

- Title 18 of the U.S. Code, Section 1960, which prohibits operating a money transmitting business without obtaining a state license, if one is required, or without registering with FinCEN.

Using publicly available documents (indictments, sentencing memoranda, law enforcement press releases, media reports, etc.), the cases were examined more closely in order to determine their key financial components. In the 229 cases surveyed, 96 included information on the financial component of the investigation, either raising or moving funds, or both. These cases were then further analyzed to determine what specific method or channel was used to raise or move funds. Despite the flaws inherent in this type of study, the data provides a revealing glimpse into TF in the United States.[7]

---

[6] *See* Department of State, Foreign Terrorist Organizations. Available at
http://www.state.gov/j/ct/rls/other/des/123085.htm.
[7] A review of case documents and follow up discussions with law enforcement and prosecutors indicates that there are a number of additional cases in which the underlying criminal conduct may have some connection to TF, but where demonstrating a nexus to terrorist activity, which is often based on classified information, is unnecessary when much of the underlying activity is already criminalized by statute (e.g., drug trafficking or fraud). As a result, the nexus to terrorist activity may not be disclosed in public charging documents or sentencing memorandum.

In addition, Bank Secrecy Act (BSA) reporting was cross-referenced with ongoing CT investigations by the FBI to provide a current picture of the risks as detected by financial institutions and shared with law enforcement.

METHODOLOGY

As in the National ML Risk Assessment, the terminology and methodology of the National TF Risk Assessment is based on the guidance of the Financial Action Task Force (FATF), the international standard-setting body for AML and CFT safeguards.[8] The FATF guidance prescribes a process for conducting a risk assessment at the national level. This approach uses the following key concepts:

- Threat: A threat is a person or group of people, or activity with the potential to cause harm to, for example, the state, society, the economy, etc. In the TF context this includes terrorist groups and their facilitators, as well as radicalized individuals that seek to exploit the United States and U.S financial system to raise and move funds. Threats are discussed in Section I.

- Vulnerability: A vulnerability is something that can be exploited to facilitate TF, both in the raising of funds for terrorist networks and the moving of funds to terrorist organizations. It may relate to a specific fundraising method or financial product used to move funds, or a weakness in regulation, supervision, or enforcement, or reflect unique circumstances in which it may be difficult to distinguish legal from illegal activity. Vulnerabilities are addressed in Section III.

- Consequence: Not all TF methods have equal consequences. The methods that allow for the greatest amount of money to be raised or moved most effectively present the greatest potential TF consequences.[9]

- Risk: Risk is a function of threat, vulnerability, and consequence.

Throughout the National TF Risk Assessment, potential TF threats, vulnerabilities and residual risks were identified, analyzed and evaluated in the following manner:

- Using the 2011 *National Strategy for Counterterrorism* and Congressional testimony from senior U.S. government officials, identifying the terrorist groups that the U.S. government has determined pose the most significant threat to the United States and the prime ways that these groups are financed, particularly where the United States and its financial system were involved;

- Cataloging the TF methods disclosed in criminal investigations and prosecutions and violations of OFAC sanctions for supporting individuals and entities designated for their support of terrorist groups;

- Analyzing financial institution reporting and cross-referencing with law enforcement CT investigations and/or OFAC designations;

---

[8] FATF Guidance, National Money Laundering and Terrorist Financing Risk Assessment, February 2013.
[9] As noted in the FATF Guidance, given the challenges in determining or estimating the consequences of TF, countries may instead opt to focus primarily on achieving a comprehensive understanding of their threats and vulnerabilities. *Id* at 8. Therefore, this National TF Risk Assessment focuses on threats and vulnerabilities in determining residual TF risks. The financing of terrorist acts and of terrorists and terrorist organizations is typically described as a three stage process requiring the raising, moving and using of funds.

- Comparing the above information with intelligence reporting to validate or refute the information;

- Assessing the extent to which domestic laws and regulations, law enforcement investigations and prosecutions, regulatory supervision, and enforcement activity and international outreach and coordination mitigate identified TF threats and vulnerabilities; and

- Using the aforementioned research and analysis to identify residual TF risks facing the United States.

The National TF Risk Assessment begins with an overview of the global terrorism threat facing the United States, the importance of financing to these organizations and their activities, and the main methods these groups use to raise and move funds.

After discussing the scope of the TF threat, the next section provides a brief overview of U.S. government efforts to mitigate the threat. This includes law enforcement efforts to investigate and prosecute terrorist supporters and legal/regulatory action to make it more difficult for terrorist financial facilitators to use the U.S. financial system.

The third section identifies the specific TF vulnerabilities in the United States that terrorist groups exploit to raise, move and place funds, the efforts made by the U.S. government to mitigate such threats and vulnerabilities, and the residual risks facing the United States and the U.S. financial system. The discussion of vulnerabilities and residual risks includes case examples from investigations and prosecutions, relevant analysis of BSA data, and preventive measures taken by the U.S. government. Despite the significant efforts invested to mitigate these vulnerabilities, residual TF risk remains.

GLOBAL TERRORIST
FINANCING THREAT

SECTION I: GLOBAL TERRORIST FINANCING THREAT

A thorough analysis of the TF risks facing the United States today first requires identifying the groups posing the most significant terrorism threat to the United States and the primary ways these groups are financed. As described in detail below, the United States faces threats from an array of terrorist groups that have gained traction in areas of instability, limited opportunity, and broken governance. They include globally oriented groups like AQ and its affiliates, as well as a growing number of regionally focused and globally connected groups. To finance their activities, these groups rely on multiple revenue streams, including criminal activity, such as kidnapping for ransom (KFR), extortion, and drug trafficking; donations directly from individuals and those funneled through charitable organizations; and state sponsorship. In addition, there is a growing threat of terrorist acts committed by radicalized individuals who are inspired by particular terrorist groups, such as AQ and the Islamic State of Iraq and the Levant (ISIL).

A. OVERVIEW OF TERRORIST THREAT FACING THE UNITED STATES

As President Obama stated in May 2014, "for the foreseeable future, the most direct threat to America at home and abroad remains terrorism."[10] But, as the President noted, the nature of the threat has changed. The threat today "comes from decentralized Al-Qaida affiliates and extremists, many with agendas focused in countries where they operate. And this lessens the possibility of large-scale [September 11, 2001]-style attacks against the homeland, but it heightens the danger of U.S. personnel overseas being attacked, as we saw in Benghazi."[11] Indeed, some terrorist groups targeting the United States may not be focused solely on directly attacking the territorial United States, but on U.S. national security interests abroad, including U.S. citizens, facilities, and allies.[12]

The U.S. government's overall counterterrorism strategy is guided by the *National Strategy for Counterterrorism*, prepared by the National Security Council. As the 2011 *National Strategy for Counterterrorism* explained, "[t]he preeminent security threat to the U.S. continues to be from Al-Qaida and its affiliates and adherents."[13] These groups have attempted several attacks on the United States, including the failed Christmas Day airline bombing in 2009, the attempted bombing of U.S.-bound cargo planes in October of 2010, and a disrupted plot to conduct a suicide bomb attack on a U.S.-bound airliner in April 2012.[14] Moreover, although the death or arrest of dozens of mid- and senior-level AQ operatives—including Osama bin Laden in May 2011—have disrupted communication, financial, and facilitation nodes, and a number of terrorist plots, the terrorist threat posed by AQ has evolved.[15]

---

[10] President Barack H. Obama, "Remarks by the President at the United States Military Academy Commencement Ceremony," May 28, 2014.
[11] *Id.*
[12] *See* White House, *National Strategy for Counterterrorism*, June 2011.
[13] *Id.*
[14] *See* James Comey, FBI Director, Testimony before the Senate Committee on Homeland Security and Governmental Affairs, "The Homeland Threat Landscape and U.S. Response," November 14, 2013. Availablehttp://www.hsgac.senate.gov/download/?id=38830fb8-ce29-4542-9748-250b69d17383.
[15] *See* Department of State, "Country Reports on Terrorism 2014," p. 374, June 2015.

Remaining members will continue to pose a threat to Western interests in South Asia and will attempt to strike the U.S. homeland should an opportunity arise.[16]

However, the threat posed by AQ extends beyond the degraded core leadership. Affiliated movements have taken root in the Middle East, East Africa, the Maghreb and Sahel regions of northwest Africa, Central Asia, and Southeast Asia. Although each group is unique, all aspire to advance AQ's regional and global agenda by destabilizing the countries in which they train and operate, attacking U.S. and other Western interests in the region, and in some cases plotting to strike the U.S. homeland.[17] For example, over the past five years, AQ in the Arabian Peninsula (AQAP) has repeatedly attempted to detonate explosives on airliners bound for the United States, while AQ in the Lands of the Islamic Maghreb (AQIM) and its allies remain focused on local and regional attack plotting, including targeting Western interests.[18] Al-Shabaab, another AQ affiliate, is mainly focused on undermining the Somali Federal Government and combating regional military forces operating in Somalia.[19] But recent attacks in Kenya, including the April 2015 attack on a college and the September 2013 attack and hostage crisis at a mall, have been linked to Al-Shabaab, and demonstrate that the group continues to support targeting regional and Western interests across East Africa.[20]

The ongoing conflict in Syria and Iraq is reshaping the nature of the terrorist threat. Since mid-2014, ISIL, with its ambitious vision, quick territorial expansion, extreme violence and brutality, and innovative use of social media, has rapidly risen to challenge AQ for primacy within the global terrorist movement. ISIL has exploited the conflict in Syria and sectarian tensions in Iraq to entrench itself in both countries. The group's strength and expansionist agenda pose an ongoing threat to U.S. regional allies and to U.S. facilities and personnel in both the Middle East and the West.[21] Along with the threat posed by ISIL, Syria and Iraq have also become magnets for over 22,500 foreign terrorist fighters, and the preeminent location for independent or AQ-aligned groups to recruit, train, and equip these individuals, including more than 180 U.S. persons and at least 4,000 Westerners.[22] Compounding the threat, veteran AQ fighters have travelled to Syria to take advantage of the permissive operating environment and easy

---

[16] Matthew G. Olsen, Director of the National Counterterrorism Center, Testimony before the Senate Committee on Homeland Security and Governmental Affairs, "The Homeland Threat Landscape and U.S. Response," November 14, 2013, http://www.hsgac.senate.gov/download/?id=4832a095-4fb4-4686-a689-0e14fc665ce9.

[17] White House, *National Strategy for Counterterrorism*, June 2011.

[18] *See* Matthew G. Olsen, Director of the National Counterterrorism Center, Testimony before the Senate Committee on Homeland Security and Governmental Affairs, "The Homeland Threat Landscape and U.S. Response," November 14, 2013.

[19] *See id.*

[20] *See id; see also* Department of State, Media Note, "Terrorist Designations of Ahmed Diriye and Mahad Karate," April 21, 2015. Available at http://www.state.gov/r/pa/prs/ps/2015/04/240932.htm.

[21] *See* Nicholas J. Rasmussen, Director, National Counterterrorism Center, Testimony before the Senate Select Committee on Intelligence titled "Current Terrorist Threats to the United States," February 12, 2015. Available at http://www.nctc.gov/docs/Current_Terrorist_Threat_to_the_United_States.pdf.

[22] *See* Nicholas J. Rasmussen, Director, National Counterterrorism Center, Testimony before the House Committee on Homeland Security "Countering Violent Islamist Extremism: The Urgent Threat of Foreign Fighters and Homegrown Terror," February 11, 2015. Available at http://www.nctc.gov/docs/Countering_Violent_Islamist_Extremism.pdf. The number of foreign terrorist fighters is updated to reflect U.S. government analysis as of May 2015.

access to foreign terrorist fighters.[23] These foreign terrorist fighters who travel to Syria and Iraq have become more radicalized, gained combat skills, made violent extremist connections, and, as demonstrated by recent attacks in Europe in early 2015, conducted organized or "lone-wolf" style attacks that target Western interests.[24] Returning foreign terrorist fighters also pose an emerging threat to the United States, as U.S. authorities have identified U.S. persons who have engaged in attack plotting following their return to the United States after traveling to and receiving military training in Syria.[25]

Beyond AQ, AQ affiliates, and ISIL, other foreign terrorist organizations threaten U.S. national security interests. These groups seek to undermine the security and stability of allied and partner governments, incite regional conflicts, traffic in drugs, or otherwise pursue agendas that are inimical to U.S. interests. In the Middle East, Hizballah remains committed to conducting terrorist activities worldwide, and the group's activities could either endanger or target U.S. and other Western interests.[26] The Islamic Resistance Movement (Hamas), which has intentionally killed hundreds of civilians, including U.S. citizens, continues to threaten U.S. interests and those of U.S. allies, notably Israel.[27]

In South Asia, Pakistani and Afghan militant groups—including Tehrik-e Taliban Pakistan (TTP), the Haqqani Network, and Lashkar-e Tayyiba (LT)—continue to pose a direct threat to U.S. interests and allies in the region, where these groups probably will remain focused.[28] TTP has carried out and claimed responsibility for numerous terrorist acts against Pakistani and U.S. interests, including a December 2009 suicide attack on a U.S. military base in Khowst, Afghanistan, which killed seven U.S. citizens, an April 2010 suicide bombing against the U.S. Consulate in Peshawar, Pakistan, which killed six Pakistani citizens, as well as the May 2010 attempted car bombing in Times Square.[29] The Haqqani Network has conducted numerous high-profile attacks against U.S., NATO, Afghan government, and other allied nation targets, and is likely to carry out additional high-profile attacks against Western interests in Afghanistan.[30] LT—the organization responsible for the rampage in Mumbai in 2008 that killed more than 150 people, including six Americans, constitutes a formidable terrorist threat to U.S. interests in

---

[23] Francis Taylor, Under Secretary for Intelligence and Analysis, Department of Homeland Security, Testimony before the House Committee on Homeland Security "Countering Violent Islamist Extremism: The Urgent Threat of Foreign Fighters and Homegrown Terror," February 11, 2015. Available at http://www.dhs.gov/news/2015/02/11/written-testimony-ia-under-secretary-house-committee-homeland-security-hearing.

[24] See James R Clapper, Director of National Intelligence, Opening Statement before the Senate Armed Services Committee "Worldwide Threat Assessment of Hearing," February 26, 2015. Available at http://www.dni.gov/files/documents/2015%20WWTA%20As%20Delivered%20DNI%20Oral%20Statement.pdf .

[25] See id; see, e.g., United States v. Abdrirahman Shiek Mohaumd, No. 2:15-cr-00095, (Indictment) (S.D. Ohio, April 16, 2015).

[26] Matthew G. Olsen, Director of the National Counterterrorism Center, Testimony before the Senate Committee on Homeland Security and Governmental Affairs, "The Homeland Threat Landscape and U.S. Response," November 14, 2013.

[27] See Department of the Treasury, Press Release, "Treasury Designates Gaza-Based Business, Television Station for Hamas Ties," March 18, 2010.

[28] Matthew G. Olsen, Director of the National Counterterrorism Center, Testimony before the Senate Committee on Homeland Security and Governmental Affairs, "The Homeland Threat Landscape and U.S. Response," November 14, 2013.

[29] See Department of State, "Country Reports on Terrorism 2014," p.385, June 2015.

[30] See Matthew G. Olsen, Director of the National Counterterrorism Center, Testimony before the Senate Committee on Homeland Security and Governmental Affairs, "The Homeland Threat Landscape and U.S. Response," November 14, 2013.

South Asia and potentially elsewhere.[31] LT has attacked Western interests in South Asia, and also provides training to Pakistani and Western militants, some of whom could plot terrorist attacks in the West without direction from LT leadership.[32]

B. GLOBAL SOURCES OF TERRORIST FINANCING

In order to operate, however, each of these groups requires significant funding. While the cost of an individual terrorist attack can be quite low, maintaining a terrorist organization requires large sums. Organizations require significant funds to create and maintain an infrastructure of organizational support, to sustain an ideology of terrorism through propaganda, and to finance the ostensibly legitimate activities needed to provide a veil of legitimacy for terrorist organizations. As deceased AQ financial chief Sa'id Al-Masri put it: "without money, jihad stops."[33] Although financial activities can vary significantly among different terrorist groups, several areas of commonality exist.

1. CRIMINAL ACTIVITY

a. Kidnapping for Ransom

Terrorist groups engage in a range of criminal activity to raise needed funds. Extensive revenue from kidnapping for ransom (KFR) and other criminal activities such as extortion have permitted AQ affiliates and other terrorist groups to generate significant revenue.[34] KFR remains one of the most frequent and profitable source of illicit financing, and an extremely challenging TF threat to combat.[35] The U.S. government estimates that terrorist organizations collected approximately $120 million in ransom payments between 2005 and 2012.[36] In 2014 alone, ISIL acquired at least $20 million and as much as $45 million in ransom payments.[37] In addition, AQAP, AQIM, and Boko Haram are particularly effective with KFR and are using ransom money to fund the range of their activities. Kidnapping targets are usually Western citizens of countries with governments that have established a pattern of paying ransoms, either directly or through third party intermediaries, for the release of individuals in custody.[38] AQAP used ransom money it received for the return of European hostages to finance its over $20 million

---

[31] White House, *National Strategy for Counterterrorism*, June 2011.

[32] *See* Matthew G. Olsen, Director of the National Counterterrorism Center, Testimony before the Senate Committee on Homeland Security and Governmental Affairs, "The Homeland Threat Landscape and U.S. Response," November 14, 2013.

[33] Daniel L. Glaser, Assistant Secretary for Terrorist Financing, Department of the Treasury, Testimony before the House Financial Services Subcommittee on Oversight and Investigations, September 6, 2011. Available at http://www.treasury.gov/press-center/press-releases/Pages/tg1287.aspx. The speeches and testimony of Treasury officials cited in the National TF Risk Assessment contain information that is derived from U.S. government analysis.

[34] *See* Department of State, "Country Reports on Terrorism 2014," pp. 9, 158, June 2015.

[35] *See* David Cohen, Under Secretary for Terrorism and Financial Intelligence, Department of the Treasury, Remarks before the Center for a New American Security, "Confronting New Threats in Terrorist Financing,'" March 4, 2014. Available at http://www.treasury.gov/press-center/press-releases/Pages/jl2308.aspx.

[36] David Cohen, Under Secretary for Terrorism and Financial Intelligence, Department of the Treasury, Remarks at Chatham House, "Kidnapping for Ransom: The Growing Terrorist Financing Challenge," October 5, 2012. Available at http://www.treasury.gov/press-center/press-releases/Pages/tg1726.aspx.

[37] Derived from U.S. government analysis.

[38] *See* Department of State, "Country Reports on Terrorism 2014," p. 377, June 2015.

campaign to seize territory in Yemen between mid-2011 and mid-2012.[39] AQIM is believed to have obtained a €30 million ransom payment in October 2013 for the release of four French hostages who worked for the French government-owned nuclear firm Areva.[40] Also in 2013, Boko Haram kidnapped eight French citizens in northern Cameroon and obtained a substantial ransom payment for their release.[41] Similarly, Al-Shabaab-affiliated groups received an approximately five million dollar ransom in exchange for the release of two Spanish hostages who were kidnapped in Kenya in October 2011.[42]

b. Extortion

The exploitation of local populations and resources has become a key revenue source for numerous terrorist groups worldwide. Pioneered by groups such as Hamas and Al-Shabaab, this form of pseudo-sovereignty-based fundraising has spread to other un- or under-governed territories around the world, most recently Iraq and Syria. Not only does territorial occupation allow for fundraising from the theft of natural resources, but it also creates the opportunity to extort, under the threat of violence, local populations and businesses and generate funds from the seizure of public utility services and their accompanying revenues. Unlike taxation by local governing authorities, whereby tax revenue is used to pay for basic public services, terrorist groups extort funds from local populations with minimal corresponding provision of services in exchange, and under the threat of physical harm for non-payment. For example, Al-Shabaab, Al-Nusrah Front (ANF) and ISIL are all able to leverage their occupation of territory and the threat of violence to extort funds from the local population, as well as conduct criminal activity such as robbery and trafficking in stolen goods. ISIL generates significant revenue, up to several million dollars per week, from the sale of stolen and smuggled energy resources it controls inside Iraq and Syria.[43] ISIL also operates sophisticated extortion rackets throughout Iraq and Syria, including extracting payments for the use of public highways and cash withdrawals from banks by depositors in cities such as Mosul.[44] Through these schemes, ISIL can receive upwards of several million dollars a month of revenue.[45] Despite losing control of the port of Kismayo, which was its key revenue source, Al-Shabaab continues to generate at least hundreds of thousands of dollars per month, primarily through extortion and the threat of violence, in its remaining strongholds in southern Somalia.[46] Similarly, Hamas can also raise revenue from control of border crossings and avenues of commerce, as well as businesses and local populations.[47]

---

[39] David Cohen, Under Secretary for Terrorism and Financial Intelligence, Department of the Treasury, Remarks before the Center for a New American Security, "Confronting New Threats in Terrorist Financing,'" March 4, 2014.

[40] *Id.*

[41] *See* Department of State, "Country Reports on Terrorism 2014," p.341, June 2015.

[42] *See* David Cohen, Under Secretary for Terrorism and Financial Intelligence, Department of the Treasury, Remarks before the Center for a New American Security, "Confronting New Threats in Terrorist Financing,'" March 4, 2014.

[43] David Cohen, Under Secretary for Terrorism and Financial Intelligence, Department of the Treasury, Testimony before the House Committee on Financial Services, "The Islamic State and Terrorist Financing" November 13, 2014. Available at http://financialservices house.gov/uploadedfiles/hhrg-113-ba00-wstate-dcohen-20141113.pdf.

[44] *Id.*

[45] *Id.*

[46] David Cohen, Under Secretary for Terrorism and Financial Intelligence, Department of the Treasury, Remarks before the Center for a New American Security, "Confronting New Threats in Terrorist Financing," March 4, 2014.

[47] Derived from U.S. government analysis.

c. Drug trafficking and other criminal activity

In addition, various terrorist groups derive significant financial benefit from other criminal activities, including through drug trafficking. Both the Revolutionary Armed Forces of Colombia (FARC) and the Taliban have utilized drug trafficking operations to finance their terrorist operations.[48] The Haqqani Network is also financed by a wide range of revenue sources including businesses and proceeds derived from criminal activities such as smuggling, extortion, and KFR in Afghanistan and Pakistan.[49] Hizballah supporters are often engaged in a range of criminal activities that benefit the group financially, such as smuggling contraband goods, passport falsification, drug trafficking, money laundering, and a variety of fraudulent schemes, including credit card, immigration, and bank fraud.[50] BSA reporting specifically implicates individuals currently being investigated by the FBI for ties to Hizballah and Hamas in a wide variety of money laundering activity within the U.S. financial system, most prominently trade-based money laundering (TBML) activities including through the export of used cars.[51]

2. *PRIVATE DONATIONS AND MISUSE OF CHARITABLE[52] ORGANIZATIONS*

Private donations from individuals and charitable organizations have continued to provide terrorist groups with a consistent flow of funds. Private donations from individuals in the Persian Gulf remained a major source of funding for several Sunni terrorist groups, particularly for those operating in Syria, as charitable fundraising networks in the Gulf have collected hundreds of millions of dollars through regular fundraising events held at homes or mosques and through social media pleas.[53] In particular, fundraisers operating in more permissive jurisdictions in the Gulf—particularly in Kuwait and Qatar—solicit donations ultimately destined for terrorist groups, including ANF.[54] These networks then use couriers, wire transfers, hawalas, and exchange houses to move those funds to Syria, often to extremists.[55] Some of this fundraising activity has occurred under the auspices of charitable giving and has involved the use of social media to reach potential donors.[56] Regarding ISIL, as the State Department noted in August 2014, "private fundraising networks increasingly rely upon social media to solicit donations and communicate

---

[48] *See* Hearing before the House Committee on Foreign Affairs, Subcommittee on Terrorism, Nonproliferation and Trade, "Narcoterrorism and the Long Reach of U.S. Law Enforcement, Part II," November 17, 2011. Available at http://www.gpo.gov/fdsys/pkg/CHRG-112hhrg71265/html/CHRG-112hhrg71265 htm.

[49] Derived from U.S. government analysis.

[50] Department of State, "Country Reports on Terrorism 2014," p.351, June 2015.

[51] Information derived from an analysis of financial institution BSA reporting cross-referenced with law enforcement investigations.

[52] The term "charitable" as used herein is intended in its broadest sense, to include charitable, humanitarian, religious, educational, and other organizations and philanthropic individuals, and unless otherwise indicated, is not limited to organizations that the IRS has determined are tax-exempt charitable organizations under Section 501(c)(3) of the Internal Revenue Code (IRC).

[53] *See* Department of State, "Country Reports on Terrorism 2014," p.373, June 2015.

[54] *See* David Cohen, Under Secretary for Terrorism and Financial Intelligence, Department of the Treasury, Remarks before the Center for a New American Security, "Confronting New Threats in Terrorist Financing,'" March 4, 2014.

[55] *Id.*

[56] *See* Department of the Treasury, Press Release, "Treasury Designates Three Key Supporters of Terrorists in Syria and Iraq," August 6, 2014. Available at http://www.treasury.gov/press-center/press-releases/Pages/jl2605.aspx. For example, Shafi Sultan Mohammed al-Ajmi, one of the designated individuals, operates regular social media campaigns seeking donations for Syrian fighters and is one of the most active Kuwaiti fundraisers for ANF. In July 2014, he publicly admitted that he collected money under the auspices of charity and delivered the funds in person to ANF.

with donors and recipient opposition groups or terrorist organizations."[57]

For funding, AQ receives donations from like-minded supporters as well as from individuals who believe that their money is supporting a humanitarian cause.[58] Some funds have also been diverted from Islamic charitable organizations.[59] In past years, they received the majority of their funds from sympathizers in the Persian Gulf, followed by supporters based in Pakistan and Turkey.[60]

LT receives the majority of its funds from within Pakistan, including by using its charitable front organizations, Jamaat-ud-Dawa (JUD) and Falah-i-Insaniyat Foundation (FIF), to solicit donations.[61] As is the case with other terrorist groups, LT generates additional funds from private donations and commercial ventures.[62] The group's two largest financial hauls come from private donations during Ramadan and profits associated with the collection and sale of animal skins during the Eid-ul-Adha holiday, each of which nets the group millions of dollars.[63]

In addition to private donations from the Persian Gulf, the provision of financial support from witting and unwitting members of key diaspora communities worldwide has also been a source of revenue for numerous terrorist groups. For example, because Al-Shabaab is a multi-clan entity, it receives donations from individuals in the Somali diaspora; however, the donations are not always intended to support terrorism, but also to support family members.[64] Similarly, Hizballah receives financial support from Lebanese Shia communities in Europe, Africa, South America, North America, and Asia, and Hamas receives donations from Palestinian expatriates around the world, including in the United States, through its charities, such as the umbrella fundraising organization, the Union of Good.[65]

3. *STATE SPONSORSHIP*

Despite ongoing diplomatic efforts and economic sanctions by the United States and its allies, some states continue to directly fund terrorist groups. Iran continues to provide Hizballah with hundreds of millions

---

[57] Marie Harf, Deputy Spokesperson, Department of State, Daily Press Briefing, August 21, 2014. Available at http://www.state.gov/r/pa/prs/dpb/2014/08/230798.htm#ISIL. In the case of ISIL, external donations raised from individuals have been used to facilitate the travel of foreign terrorist fighters to Syria and Iraq. *See* FATF, Financing of the Terrorist Organization Islamic State in Iraq and the Levant, February 2015.

[58] Department of State, "Country Reports on Terrorism 2014," p.375, June 2015.

[59] *Id.*

[60] *See* David Cohen, Under Secretary for Terrorism and Financial Intelligence, Department of the Treasury, Remarks before the Center for a New American Security, "Confronting New Threats in Terrorist Financing,'" March 4, 2014.

[61] Derived from U.S. government analysis. LT coordinates charitable activities through its U.S.- and UN-designated front organizations, JUD, which spearheaded humanitarian relief to the victims of the October 2005 earthquake in Kashmir, and FIF, which was widely reported to have provided aid to flood victims in Pakistan in 2010. To raise awareness regarding this activity, as well as to provide guidance as to how charities and donors can avoid directly or indirectly providing assistance to terrorist organizations, Treasury issued specific guidance in the wake of the October 2005 earthquake, which is available at http://www.treasury.gov/resource-center/terrorist-illicit-finance/Documents/charities_post-earthquake.pdf.

[62] Derived from U.S. government analysis.

[63] *Id.*

[64] Department of State, "Country Reports on Terrorism 2014," p.384, June 2015.

[65] *Id.* at 346, 351.

of dollars in aid each year, which makes up a significant portion of the group's funding.[66] As with Hizballah, state sponsorship has played a significant role in Hamas' financing. Historically, Hamas has received funding, weapons, and training from Iran, but the relationship suffered after Hamas refused to follow Iran's lead in supporting Syrian President Bashar al-Asad.[67]

As described above, the terrorist organizations that pose a threat to the United States employ a variety of methods to raise funds necessary to carry out terrorist acts. To combat these groups and the threat they pose, the U.S. government has developed and implemented a comprehensive CT strategy, which includes disrupting financing for these terrorist organizations. Domestically, several U.S. government agencies play critical roles in the effort to combat TF in the United States. Section II provides an overview of the interagency effort to disrupt domestic sources of TF.

---

[66] Derived from U.S. government analysis.
[67] *See* Department of State, "Country Reports on Terrorism 2014," p.285, June 2015.

COUNTERING
TERRORIST
FINANCING

SECTION II: COUNTERING TERRORIST FINANCING

Although all of the groups in Section I pose threats to U.S. national security interests, every TF method they employ does not necessarily pose an immediate TF risk in the United States. After the September 11, 2001 terrorist attacks, the U.S. government aligned its efforts to prevent future terrorist attacks. As President Obama recently noted, in the wake of the September 11, 2001 terrorist attacks "we demanded that our intelligence community improve its capabilities, and that law enforcement change practices to focus more on preventing attacks before they happen than prosecuting terrorists after an attack."[68]

Prevention and early detection is at the core of U.S. government threat mitigation efforts and remains the U.S. government's top priority. Preventing terrorists from raising, moving, placing and using funds is central to this effort. As noted in the 2011 *National Strategy for Counterterrorism*, one of the U.S. government's eight overarching CT goals is to deprive terrorists of their enabling means, which includes financial support, by expanding and enhancing "efforts aimed at blocking the flow of financial resources to and among terrorist groups and to disrupt terrorist facilitation and support activities, imposing sanctions or pursuing prosecutions to enforce violations and dissuade others." These efforts fall into three broad categories: (i) law enforcement efforts; (ii) financial/regulatory measures; and (iii) international engagement.

A. LAW ENFORCEMENT EFFORTS

The ongoing work of the law enforcement agencies (LEAs) has been and remains central to U.S. CFT efforts. Since the September 11, 2001 terrorist attacks, LEAs have undertaken a fundamental reorientation of their institutions, processes, resources, and apparatuses to enhance their ability to disrupt and prevent acts of terrorism before they occur.[69] The DOJ, the principal government entity responsible for overseeing the investigation and prosecution of TF offenses at the federal level, uses its authorities to investigate and dismantle terrorist financiers and thus deter future supporters.[70] To advance this mission and in recognition of the importance of tracking the financial underpinnings of terrorist activity, FBI-TFOS was established immediately after September 11, 2001 to identify and disrupt all TF activities.[71] FBI-TFOS is charged with managing FBI's investigative efforts into TF facilitators and ensuring financial investigative techniques are used, where appropriate, in all FBI CT investigations to enhance the investigations.[72] For example, to the extent that funds affiliated with individuals being investigated by the FBI for ties to AQ and other terrorist groups still transit through the U.S. financial system, FBI and its law enforcement partners make extensive use of Suspicious Activity Reports (SARs) and Currency

---

[68] President Obama, "Remarks by the President on Review of Signals Intelligence," 1/17/2014. Available at http://www.whitehouse.gov/the-press-office/2014/01/17/remarks-president-review-signals-intelligence.

[69] *See generally* Department of Justice, "FY 2013 Annual Performance Report and FY 2015 Annual Performance Plan," March 2014.

[70] *See* Office of the Inspector General, Department of Justice, "Audit of the Federal Bureau of Investigation's and the National Security Division's Efforts to Coordinate and Address Terrorist Financing," Audit Report 13-17, March 2013. Available at http://www.justice.gov/oig/reports/2013/a1317.pdf.

[71] *See id.*

[72] Ralph S. Boelter, Acting Assistant Director, FBI Counterterrorism Division, Statement Before the Senate Judiciary Committee, Subcommittee on Crime and Terrorism, September 21, 2011.

Transaction Reports (CTRs) related to TF in order to interdict and seize such funds.[73] FBI-TFOS works in close coordination with the National Joint Terrorism Task Force (JTTF), which coordinates CT efforts of federal, state and local law enforcement agencies through local JTTFs in 104 cities nationwide, foreign partners, and the financial industry. These efforts have reduced the funding available for terrorist operations and have made the concealment and transfer of terrorism related funds more difficult.[74] In addition to FBI-TFOS, other DOJ components play a key role in TF investigations. DEA's drug trafficking and money laundering enforcement initiatives seek to deny drug trafficking and money laundering routes to terrorist organizations, while the Bureau of Alcohol, Tobacco, Firearms and Explosives (ATF) investigates the illegal sale of explosives and tobacco products.[75] When an investigation produces sufficient evidence for a criminal prosecution, the U.S. Attorneys' Offices, working closely with the DOJ's National Security and Criminal Divisions, leverage multiple federal criminal statutes to prosecute cases involving TF.

In addition to the DOJ, other LEAs play important roles in furthering U.S. CFT efforts. Within DHS, Customs and Border Protection (CBP) detects the movement of bulk cash across U.S. borders and maintains data about the movement of commodities and persons in and out of the United States, while Immigration and Customs Enforcement-Homeland Security Investigations (ICE-HSI) initiates investigations of terrorist financing involving transnational crimes to include smuggling and TBML. The IRS, a bureau within Treasury which administers and enforces U.S. tax laws, also plays a supporting role in the U.S. government's CFT efforts, in particular through the work of IRS-CI, which investigates criminal violations of U.S. tax law, as well as money laundering and other financial crimes, and IRS-TE/GE, which administers IRS regulations related to tax-exempt charitable organizations.[76] When authorized to assist in a TF investigation, these IRS components can provide unique expertise and authorities to support U.S. government CFT efforts.

These efforts are supported by the financial intelligence and analytical work of FinCEN. FinCEN grants more than 10,000 agents, analysts, and investigative personnel from more than 350 agencies across the U.S. government direct access to BSA reporting. There are about 30,000 searches of the data taking place daily. This financial intelligence allows LEAs to identify significant relationships, patterns and trends. The reporting unmasks the relationships between possible terrorist groups and their financing networks, enabling law enforcement to target the underlying conduct of concern, and to use forfeiture and sanctions to disrupt their ability to operate and finance their activities.

The significant number of TF cases brought by various LEAs and the whole of government approach exemplifies the active role LEAs take in prosecuting terrorist support networks. Since 2001, more than 229 cases have either led to convictions or are still pending judgment against individuals who were charged with supporting—or conspiring to support—terrorism or terrorist groups through material support, transmitting money without a license, narco-terrorism, and economic sanctions violations.

---

[73] Information derived from an analysis of financial institution BSA reporting cross-referenced with law enforcement investigations.

[74] *Id.*

[75] DEA, Department of Justice, "FY 2014 Performance Budget Congressional Submission." Available at http://www.justice.gov/jmd/2014justification/pdf/dea-justification.pdf.

[76] *See* IRS, Department of the Treasury: "The Budget in Brief: Internal Revenue Service FY 2015."

B. FINANCIAL/REGULATORY EFFORTS

As part of the broader post-September 11, 2001 CT efforts, the U.S. government focused increasingly on the importance of disrupting the finances and funding networks that fueled terrorist organizations and on the importance of financial intelligence collected and disseminated by domestic financial institutions.[77] Treasury's Office of Terrorism and Financial Intelligence (TFI) was established in 2004 to lead the U.S. government's CFT efforts.[78] TFI seeks to mitigate TF risk through both systemic and targeted actions. Targeted actions, usually in the form of targeted financial sanctions administered and enforced by OFAC, are used to identify, disrupt, and prevent terrorists from accessing the U.S. financial system.

These actions are complemented by the efforts of FinCEN and the federal functional regulators that evaluate and enforce a financial institution's compliance with the appropriate regulatory requirements. For example, as administrator of the BSA, FinCEN, a component of TFI, promulgates implementing regulations for the BSA to reduce the potential for abuse by various illicit finance threats, including TF. To develop these regulations FinCEN and other offices within TFI regularly engage all the appropriate stakeholders to understand these threats. FinCEN works with the federal functional regulators and law enforcement to develop guidance, administrative rulings and advisories for the financial industry to aid financial institutions in identifying priority threats such as TF.

Additionally, U.S. government CFT initiatives have benefited from and contributed to long-standing efforts to protect the financial system against all forms of illicit finance. These laws, rules, regulations and guidance have aided financial institutions in identifying and managing risk, provided valuable information to law enforcement, and created the foundation of financial transparency required to deter, detect, and punish those who would abuse the U.S. financial system to launder the proceeds of crime and move funds for illicit purposes.[79] For example, controls instituted to combat money laundering have also strengthened our ability to identify, deter, and disrupt TF.[80]

---

[77] *See* Jacob J. Lew, Secretary of the Treasury, Remarks at the Center for Strategic and International Studies, "TFI@10: The Evolution of Treasury's National Security Role," June 2, 2014. For example, as of June 2012, 37 percent of the FBI's pending CT cases had associated BSA records. David Cohen, Under Secretary for Terrorism and Financial Intelligence, Department of the Treasury, Testimony before the Senate Committee on Banking, Housing and Urban Affairs "Patterns of Abuse: Assessing Bank Secrecy Act Compliance and Enforcement," March 7, 2013. Available at http://www.treasury.gov/press-center/press-releases/Pages/jl1871.aspx.

[78] TFI is composed of: TFFC, TFI's policy development and outreach office; OFAC which is charged with administering and enforcing all U.S. economic sanctions programs, including those targeting TF; OIA, TFI's in-house intelligence office; and FinCEN, the financial intelligence unit (FIU) for the United States, which is also charged with administering and enforcing the BSA. *See* Department of the Treasury, *Organizational Structure.* Available at http://www.treasury.gov/press-center/press-releases/Pages/hp361.aspx.

[79] David Cohen, Under Secretary for Terrorism and Financial Intelligence, Department of the Treasury, Testimony before the Senate Committee on Banking, Housing and Urban Affairs "Patterns of Abuse: Assessing Bank Secrecy Act Compliance and Enforcement," March 7, 2013.

[80] Of the individuals being investigated by law enforcement for ties to terrorist organizations who has associated BSA records, 58 percent were identified in financial institution BSA reporting as having engaged in suspected money laundering, including structuring, according to information derived from an analysis of financial institution BSA reporting cross-referenced with law enforcement investigations.

C. INTERNATIONAL ENGAGEMENT

As described earlier, the scope and reach of the U.S. financial system makes it vulnerable to TF abuse. Moreover, because many of the terrorist groups and foreign terrorist fighters described above pose a direct threat to the U.S. homeland and U.S. national security interests abroad, the United States has a vested interest in disrupting their financial activity even if it never actually reaches the U.S. financial system. In recognition of this and of the increasing interconnectedness of the global financial system, a secure global framework is essential to effectively mitigate TF risk within the U.S. financial system. To that end, the U.S. government engages bilaterally and multilaterally to globalize its CFT efforts by: (i) supporting the development of strong international AML/CFT standards and working towards robust implementation of them through the FATF and the United Nations (UN) as well as other bodies; (ii) raising international awareness of the nature and characteristics of TF as well as calling attention to specific threats; and (iii) providing training and technical assistance to bolster national CFT regimes and enforcement mechanisms. Helping to strengthen global AML/CFT regimes has a direct benefit to the safety and integrity of the U.S. financial system, given the global nature of money laundering and TF and the relationships between banks abroad.[81] The U.S. government considers strong international AML/CFT regimes critical in advancing its efforts to prevent TF from touching the U.S. financial system in the first place. Moreover, this global AML/CFT architecture assists the U.S. government in systematically identifying and addressing TF vulnerabilities in the international financial system on an ongoing basis. Such a global architecture in turn enhances our ability to both protect the integrity of the international financial system and undermine the financial networks that support terrorist organizations.[82]

D. EXAMPLE OF SUCCESSFUL INTERAGENCY COORDINATION: RESPONSE TO THE ATTEMPTED TIMES SQUARE BOMBING

In addition to its focus on preventing future attacks to the homeland, in the event that a terrorist plot develops, the U.S. government makes extensive use of financial intelligence to identify, investigate, and prosecute the network involved in plotting the attack.

On May 1, 2010, Faisal Shahzad, a naturalized U.S. citizen born in Pakistan, drove a Nissan Pathfinder loaded with explosives to Times Square, began the detonation process and fled the Pathfinder. A street vendor noticed smoke coming from the Pathfinder and alerted police, who evacuated Times Square and sent in the bomb squad. Following the attempted attack, multiple U.S. government agencies rapidly coordinated an expansive investigation into the potential suspects. On May 3, 2010, Shahzad was pulled off a flight at JFK airport set to depart for Dubai by the Department of Homeland Security. Shahzad received explosives training in Waziristan, Pakistan from explosive trainers affiliated with TTP.[83] In June

---

[81] David Cohen, Under Secretary for Terrorism and Financial Intelligence, Department of the Treasury, Testimony before the Senate Committee on Homeland Security and Governmental Affairs Permanent Subcommittee on Investigations, "U.S. Vulnerabilities to Money Laundering, Drugs, and Terrorist Financing: HSBC Case History," July 17, 2012. Available at http://www.hsgac.senate.gov/download/?id=55d94bbb-cbee-4a35-89ca-5493a12d73dd.
[82] See Daniel L. Glaser, Assistant Secretary for Terrorist Financing, Department of the Treasury, Testimony before the U.S.-China Economic and Security Review Commission, Hearing on Macau and Hong Kong, June 27, 2013. Available at http://www.uscc.gov/sites/default/files/Glaser%20Testimony.pdf.
[83] See FBI, Press Release, "Faisal Shahzad Pleads Guilty in Manhattan Federal Court to 10 Federal Crimes Arising from Attempted Car Bombing in Times Square," June 21, 2010.

2010, Shahzad pleaded guilty to ten counts, and in October 2010 he was sentenced to life in prison without possibility of parole.[84]

A review and analysis of financial records and information provided to law enforcement by financial institutions played a key role in the investigation, successful identification, and prosecution of Shahzad, including his link to TTP. To fund the bombing, Shahzad in February 2010 received about $4,900 in cash (sent from a TTP supporter in Pakistan) in Massachusetts, which he picked up from a gas station attendant named Aftab Ali Khan acting as a unlicensed money transmitter.[85] Six weeks later, he received another $7,000 in cash (sent by the same conspirator in Pakistan) in Ronkonkoma, New York, from a Pakistani businessman named Mohammed Younis who was also acting as an unlicensed money transmitter.[86] Khan pleaded guilty to immigration and unlicensed money transmitter charges and was deported to Pakistan in May 2011. Younis pleaded guilty to operating as an unlicensed money transmitter in August 2011 was sentenced to 3 years' probation and ordered to forfeit $12,000.

---

[84] *See* FBI, Press Release, "Faisal Shahzad Sentenced in Manhattan Federal Court to Life in Prison for Attempted Car Bombing in Times Square," October 5, 2010.
[85] *See* FBI, Press Release, "Pakistani Man Sentenced on Unlicensed Money Transmitting and Immigration Fraud Charges," April 11, 2011.
[86] *See United States v. Mohammad Younis*, 10 Cr. 813 (Sentencing Memorandum), (S.D.N.Y. filed November 23, 2011).

TERRORIST FINANCING VULNERABILITIES AND RISKS IN THE UNITED STATES

SECTION III: TERRORIST FINANCING
VULNERABILITIES AND RISKS IN THE UNITED STATES

This section is intended to expand upon the specific vulnerabilities that terrorist organizations and radicalized individuals can exploit to raise, move, and place funds, and which the U.S. government has determined pose a residual risk to the United States and U.S. financial system. The United States faces residual risk from vulnerabilities associated with criminal activity, including narcotics trafficking and other criminal acts, misuse of charitable organizations and individuals raising funds under the auspices of charitable giving, and direct financial support from individuals to terrorist organizations. As noted above, in part due to the central role of U.S. financial institutions in the international financial system and the attractiveness of the U.S. dollar as a globally accepted medium of exchange, the United States faces some residual TF risk from vulnerabilities associated with various types of regulated and unregulated financial institutions, as well as cash smuggling, which are being addressed through ongoing U.S. government outreach, regulation, and law enforcement activities. Additionally, the U.S. government continues to monitor emerging TF threats and vulnerabilities, including the use of cybercrime and identify theft schemes by terrorist groups to raise funds, as well at the use of new payment systems to move and place funds.

A. RAISING FUNDS: VULNERABILITIES AND RISKS

1. *CRIMINAL ACTIVITY*

The U.S. government has observed that numerous terrorist organizations worldwide engage in criminal activity to fund their organizations and operations. Globally, AQ, ISIL, the Haqqani Network and ANF, for example, are known to be financed in part by proceeds derived from smuggling, robbery, and extortion.[87] Based on an analysis of U.S. criminal investigations leading to prosecutions, terrorist organizations continue to rely on criminal activities[88] in the United States to finance their operations. Of the cases reviewed, about 24 percent involved some criminal activity, such as smuggling, drug trafficking or fraud, being used to fund terrorist activity.[89]

The U.S. government has observed that both criminal organizations and terrorist groups continue to develop international networks and establish alliances of convenience.[90] Moreover, looking forward, as terrorist groups increasingly reveal a willingness to engage in criminal activities to raise funds, the risk

---

[87] Derived from U.S. government analysis.

[88] While providing funds to terrorists and terrorist organizations is itself a criminal act, regardless of the source of those funds, the reference to "criminal activity" refers to criminal acts other than providing financial support to a terrorist organization.

[89] As described above, an analysis was conducted by Treasury on terrorism and terrorism-related convictions between 2001 and 2014. Using publicly available documents (indictments, sentencing memoranda, law enforcement press releases, media reports, etc.) the cases were examined more closely in order to determine key financial components. In the 229 cases surveyed, 96 included information on the financial component to the investigation, either raising or moving the funds. These cases were then further analyzed to determine what specific method or channel was used to raise or move funds.

[90] Karen P. Tandy, Administrator, DEA, Statement Before the House Committee on Armed Services U.S. House of Representatives, "Status of Security and Stability in Afghanistan," June 28, 2006. Available at http://www.dea.gov/pr/speeches-testimony/2006t/ct062806p.html.

that they will collaborate with international criminal organizations increases.[91] Collaboration can serve as a force multiplier for both criminal and terrorist groups, bolstering their capabilities, strengthening their infrastructure, and increasing their wealth. Often, the potential profits associated with criminal activity are a motivating factor for both organized crime and terrorist groups.[92]

To the extent that this criminal activity occurs in the United States, it is subject to a range of U.S. government action including targeted financial sanctions and law enforcement actions. Although the FBI is the lead investigative agency for material support-related investigations as well as for those cases in which criminal activity is used as a TF method, the DEA plays a significant role in those cases that involve drug trafficking. Given the substantial resources the U.S. government commits to combating the threat posed by transnational organized crime, other U.S. government agencies also support these TF investigations where there is a nexus with particular types of transnational organized crime, such as cross-border smuggling of goods.[93] As with all TF-related activity, DOJ attorneys prosecute these cases. Although the number of TF prosecutions for such activity in the United States may be relatively lower than for other types of activity, criminal activity remains a residual TF risk in part due to the high-revenue nature of the activity.[94] For example, although an individual terrorist financier raising money under the auspices of charitable giving may provide hundreds or thousands of dollars' worth of material support, the benefit provided to a terrorist organization from drug trafficking activity may be significantly greater, and a single KFR payment can run into the millions. Cases included in this section, for example, involve the movement of multi-ton quantities of drugs either belonging to or for the benefit of terrorists and the smuggling of hundreds of thousands of dollars' worth of electronics and cash.

a. Kidnapping for Ransom

As discussed in Section I, the magnitude and scale of terrorists relying on criminal proceeds has reached new heights with the spread of KFR as a fundraising strategy. KFR has become one of the most frequent and profitable sources of TF.[95] Despite the significant TF risk posed by KFR globally, abuse of the U.S. financial system to KFR-related TF is relatively low. As a matter of long-standing policy, the U.S. government does not pay ransoms or make other concessions to terrorist organizations holding U.S. citizens hostage.[96]

---

[91] David Cohen, Assistant Secretary for Terrorist Financing, Remarks to the ABA/ABA Money Laundering Enforcement Conference, October 12, 2009. Available at http://www.treasury.gov/press-center/press-releases/Pages/tg317.aspx.

[92] *See id.*

[93] *See* White House, *Strategy to Combat Transnational Organized Crime: Addressing Converging Threats to National Security*, July 2011.

[94] The lower number of prosecutions for criminal activity in support of terrorist financing may be due to the fact that demonstrating a nexus to terrorist activity, which is often based on classified information, is unnecessary where much of the underlying activity is already criminalized by statute (e.g. drug trafficking or fraud), and thus the nexus to terrorist activity may not be disclosed in public charging documents or sentencing memorandum.

[95] Department of State, Fact Sheet "Country Reports on Terrorism 2013," April 30, 2014. Available at http://www.state.gov/r/pa/prs/ps/2014/04/225406.htm.

[96] *See* White House, Office of the Press Secretary, Press Briefing by the Press Secretary, November 18, 2014. Available at https://www.whitehouse.gov/the-press-office/2014/11/18/press-briefing-press-secretary-11182014.

However, given the significant TF risk globally of KFR, the U.S. government has focused its efforts internationally, using a multifaceted approach to prevent terrorist groups from successfully using kidnapping to raise money. These efforts focus primarily on (i) preventing kidnappings, (ii) reducing the incentive to take hostages by encouraging governments to refrain from making concessions to terrorists, and (iii) denying terrorist kidnappers the benefits of their crime by working with international partners to locate, arrest and prosecute hostage takers and locate, freeze, and recover their assets. These efforts in coordination with international partners have resulted in a number of multilateral initiatives on KFR.[97] Despite these efforts, KFR continues to be a significant TF risk globally. Thus, the U.S. government will continue to engage global partners and the private sector to endeavor to reduce the availability of KFR as a source of TF.

b. Drug Trafficking

Another lucrative criminal activity that has benefited some terrorist organizations is drug trafficking. As demonstrated by a review of publicly available information on U.S. law enforcement cases (particularly investigations led by the DEA) involving terrorism and TF offenses and financial and intelligence reporting, ongoing links between drug trafficking networks and terrorist organizations and their facilitators continue to present a residual TF risk to the United States through "narco-terrorism." Approximately seven percent of the TF-related law enforcement cases reviewed involved drug smuggling.[98] Illicit drugs have long been attractive commodities to smuggle due to their high pecuniary value, as well as the ease with which they can be appropriated, processed, stored, and transported. Additionally, despite the success of various U.S. government initiatives in combating illegal drug sales and use domestically, the United States continues to be a source of demand for the global drug trade.[99]

Multiple terrorist groups have benefited from the global drug trade and drug sales to the United States to finance their operations. In one case, a group of drug traffickers in West Africa agreed to receive and store multi-ton shipments of Taliban-owned heroin in Benin and to transport the heroin to Ghana, from where they understood portions of the heroin would be sent on a commercial airplane to the United States to be sold for the financial benefit of the Taliban.[100] The case also demonstrates the nexus between narco-trafficking and other forms of material support, such as weapons trafficking. The links between drug traffickers and terrorist facilitators can extend beyond a single terrorist organization. Several of these same drug traffickers agreed to arrange the sale of weapons for the Taliban's use in Afghanistan, and indicated they also facilitated weapons trafficking for Hizballah.[101]

---

[97] For example, UN Security Council Resolution 2199, passed in February 2015, reaffirmed (1) previous calls on states to prevent terrorists from benefiting from ransom payments or from political concessions; (2) that UN sanctions prohibit ransom payments to UN-listed groups (including ISIL and ANF); and (3) the need for states to cooperate closely during kidnapping incidents. UN Security Council Resolution 2199 (2015). Available at http://www.un.org/press/en/2015/sc11775.doc.htm. Additionally, the multinational Counter-ISIL Financing Group identified as one of its key objectives denying ISIL the use of KFR as a source of revenue. *See* Department of State, Media Note, "Establishment of the Counter-ISIL Finance Group in Rome, Italy," March 20, 2015.

[98] *See* Footnote 89.

[99] *See* White House, Office of National Drug Control Policy, *National Drug Control Strategy*, p.35, 2014.

[100] *See United States v. Saade et al.*, Case No. 1:11-cr-00111 (Indictment) (S.D.N.Y. February 2011).

[101] *See id.*

In another case, a drug trafficker agreed to arrange the importation of hundreds of kilograms of high-quality heroin into the United States and was led to believe that the profits would be used, among other things, to purchase weapons for Hizballah.[102] Another individual also arranged for the sale of six assault rifles and an additional 10 kilograms of heroin that he believed was destined for the United States, and would fund the Taliban from the proceeds of the sale of the heroin.[103]

In accordance with overall CT/CFT priorities, the United States takes a proactive approach to combating the TF vulnerability posed by narco-terrorism, including through sting operations and aggressive prosecutions under post-September 11, 2001 authorities. The USA PATRIOT Act which, with related successor bills, significantly augmented DEA's authority in narco-terrorism investigations and prosecutions, specifically in regards to 21 U.S.C. § 959 and § 960a.[104] 21 U.S.C. § 959 expands the reach of DEA to acts of manufacture or distribution outside of the United States.[105] This section makes it unlawful for any person to manufacture or distribute a controlled substance or listed chemical intending or knowing that it will be unlawfully imported into the United States.[106] 21 U.S.C. § 960a allows for prosecution of terrorist-related, extra-territorial drug offenses and provides DOJ with a particularly powerful tool to prosecute, disrupt, and dismantle narco-terrorist groups worldwide.[107] Of the cases surveyed since 2006, there have been 17 cases in which an alleged narco-terrorist has been indicted or convicted of drug-related crimes or for providing direct material support to a terrorist organization.[108] These individuals were associated with a variety of terrorist organizations, including the FARC, Hizballah, AQ, and the Taliban.[109] In 12 of these 17 cases, the individuals were also charged with providing material support to terrorist groups.[110]

DEA enforcement efforts work to disrupt and dismantle entire drug trafficking networks by targeting their leaders for arrest and prosecution, confiscating the profits that fund continuing drug operations, and eliminating international sources of supply. DEA's drug trafficking and money laundering enforcement initiatives support and augment U.S. government CT/CFT efforts by reducing the availability of drug trafficking and/or money laundering routes to terrorist organizations and by employing measures to prevent the use of illicit drugs as barter for munitions to support terrorism.[111] In order to pursue transnational narco-terrorism cases against high-level, often foreign or foreign-located targets, DEA established the Counter-Narco-Terrorism Operations Center (CNTOC) within its Special Operations Division to manage its worldwide activities.[112] CNTOC is a multi-agency section with the primary

---

[102] *See United States v. Henareh, et al.*, Case No. 1:11-cr-00093 (Indictment) (S.D.N.Y. July 2011).

[103] *See United* States v. Taza Gul Alizai, 10 Cr. 799 (Indictment) (S.D.N.Y. July 2011).

[104] *See* DEA, Department of Justice, "FY 2014 Performance Budget Congressional Submission." Available at http://www.justice.gov/sites/default/files/jmd/legacy/2014/05/16/dea-justification.pdf.

[105] *Id.*

[106] *Id.*

[107] *Id.*

[108] *See* Footnote 89.

[109] *Id.*

[110] *Id.*

[111] DEA, Department of Justice, "FY 2014 Performance Budget Congressional Submission."

[112] Derek S. Maltz, Special Agent in Charge of the Special Operations Division, DEA, Statement before the House Foreign Affairs Subcommittee on Terrorism, Non-proliferation, and Trade, "Narcoterrorism and the Long Reach of U.S. Law Enforcement, Part II," November 17, 2011. Available at http://www.justice.gov/dea/pr/speeches-testimony/2012-2009/111117_testimony.pdf.

mission of coordinating all DEA investigations and intelligence related to narco-terrorism and money laundering linked to terrorist organizations by sharing intelligence with its domestic and foreign offices.[113] It forms the central hub for addressing the increase in narco-terrorism related issues and investigations.[114] Additionally, the U.S. Attorney's Office in the Southern District of New York (USAO-SDNY) created a combined Terrorism and International Narcotics Unit to target and prosecute global transnational threats.[115] The U.S. Attorney's Office for the Eastern District of Virginia (USAO-EDVA) has also similarly restructured its office to combine units for maximum impact.[116]

The details of several publicly reported investigations and prosecutions, including for violations of 21 U.S.C. §§ 959 and 960a, exemplify how terrorist organizations generate revenue from drug trafficking as well as the proactive whole-of-government approach of the U.S. government to combat narco-terrorism globally and domestically. On June 12, 2012, an international drug trafficker was sentenced to life in prison for conspiring to distribute heroin in the United States and using drug proceeds to fund, arm, and supply the Taliban.[117] The defendant had been convicted on numerous narco-terrorism-related charges, including violations of 21 U.S.C. § 959 and § 960a. The defendant manufactured heroin in clandestine laboratories along Afghanistan's border region with Pakistan and led one of the largest heroin trafficking organizations in the world.[118] The defendant sent the drug to more than 20 countries, including the United States.[119] Proceeds from his heroin trafficking were then used to support high-level members of the Taliban in furtherance of their insurgency in Afghanistan.[120]

Another example of a terrorist organization benefiting from drug trafficking as well as from maintaining physical control over territory involves the FARC. To facilitate the movement of its cocaine into and out of FARC-controlled territory, the one defendant's organization made regular payments to the FARC.[121] On April 26, 2013, the USAO-SDNY announced the extradition from Colombia of the defendant on charges that he conspired to import ton-quantities of cocaine into the United States, to provide material support to the FARC and to engage in narco-terrorism under 21 U.S.C. § 960a.[122] The defendant, a Colombian citizen, had previously been designated a Consolidated Priority Organization Target

---

[113] *Id.*

[114] *Id.*

[115] *Id.*

[116] Derek S. Maltz, Special Agent in Charge of the Special Operations Division, DEA, Statement before the House Foreign Affairs Subcommittee on Terrorism, Non-proliferation, and Trade, "Narcoterrorism and the Long Reach of U.S. Law Enforcement, Part II," November 17, 2011. Available at http://www.justice.gov/dea/pr/speeches-testimony/2012-2009/111117_testimony.pdf.

[117] Department of Justice, Press Release, "Haji Bagcho Sentenced to Life in Prison on Drug Trafficking and Narco-Terrorism Charges," June 12, 2012.

[118] *Id.*

[119] *Id.*

[120] *See id.; see also United States v. Haji Bagcho*, Case No. 1:06-cr-00334-ESH (Sentencing Memorandum) (D.D.C. June 2012).

[121] *See United States v. Jose Evaristo Linares Castillo*, 11 Cr. 1054 (Indictment) (S.D.N.Y. March 2013).

[122] Department of Justice, Press Release, "Manhattan U.S. Attorney Announces Extradition Of Alleged International Narcotics Trafficker Charged With Conspiring To Engage In Narco-Terrorism And To Support The FARC," April 26, 2013.

(CPOT)[123] and Treasury designated him as a Specially Designated Narcotics Trafficker (SDNT) in February 2013 to build upon DEA's and DOJ's actions.[124]

U.S. law enforcement and regulators have also sought to penalize foreign financial institutions that are used to launder the proceeds of drug sales and allow terrorist organizations to benefit. For example, in January 2011, Treasury designated Lebanese drug trafficker Ayman Joumaa, as well as nine individuals and 19 entities—including three Lebanon-based exchange houses—connected to his drug trafficking and money laundering organization as SDNTs pursuant to the Foreign Narcotics Kingpin Designation Act (Kingpin Act).[125] Joumaa coordinated the transportation, distribution, and sale of multi-ton shipments of cocaine from South America and laundered the proceeds from the sale of cocaine in Europe and the Middle East.[126] Importantly, Hizballah derived financial support from the criminal activities of the Joumaa network.[127] In February 2011, Treasury followed up on these actions under the Kingpin Act by identifying Lebanese Canadian Bank SAL (LCB) as a financial institution of "primary money laundering concern" under Section 311 of the USA PATRIOT Act for the bank's role in facilitating the money laundering activities of the previously-designated Joumaa drug-trafficking and money laundering network.[128] Joumaa and his Lebanon-based drug network, along with several other individuals, used LCB to launder drug proceeds—as much as $200 million per month – as part of its international money laundering network. The proceeds were laundered through various methods, including bulk cash smuggling operations and use of several Lebanese exchange houses that utilize accounts at LCB branches.[129] LCB managers were also linked to Hizballah officials outside of Lebanon.[130]

These targeted financial measures paved the way for additional actions taken by DOJ, which used its authorities to go after relevant assets it could target with law enforcement tools. In December 2011, Joumaa was indicted by the USAO-EDVA.[131] Additionally, in December 2011, the USAO-SDNY filed a civil complaint seeking forfeiture of the assets of both the financial institutions involved in Joumaa's scheme (including LCB) and approximately 30 U.S. car buyers and a U.S. shipping company that

---

[123] The CPOT List is a multi-agency target list of "command and control" elements of the most prolific international drug trafficking and money laundering organizations.

[124] *See* Department of Justice, Press Release, "Manhattan U.S. Attorney Announces Extradition Of Alleged International Narcotics Trafficker Charged With Conspiring To Engage In Narco-Terrorism And To Support The FARC," April 26, 2013. Under E.O. 12978, an individual can be designated a SDNT and, as a result, have his/her property and interests in the U.S. blocked, for meeting the following criteria: plays a significant role in international drug trafficking centered in Colombia; materially assists in, or provide s financial or technological support for or goods or services in support of, the drug trafficking activities of SDNTs; or is owned or controlled by, or act s for or on behalf of, any other SDNT.

[125] Department of the Treasury, Press Release, "Treasury Targets Major Lebanese-Based Drug Trafficking and Money Laundering Network," January 26, 2011.

[126] *See* FinCEN, *Finding That the Lebanese Canadian Bank SAL Is a Financial Institution of Primary Money Laundering Concern*," Notice of Finding, 76 Fed. Reg. 9403, February 17, 2011.

[127] *Id.*

[128] *Id.*

[129] *Id.*

[130] FinCEN, *Finding That the Lebanese Canadian Bank SAL Is a Financial Institution of Primary Money Laundering Concern*," Notice of Finding, 76 Fed. Reg. 9403, February 17, 2011.

[131] *United States* v. Joumaa, Case No. 1:11-cr-00560 (Indictment) (E.D. Va. November 2011).

facilitated the scheme, as the proceeds of violations of IEEPA and of money laundering offenses.[132] As part of a settlement, LCB was ordered to forfeit $102 million to the U.S. government.[133] Treasury continued to pursue this network with additional Section 311 actions in April 2013 against two Lebanese exchange houses—Kassem Rmeiti & Co. For Exchange and Halawi Exchange Co.—which continued the Joumaa network's money laundering work, including TBML schemes involving used car dealerships in the United States and consumer goods from Asia, after Treasury's actions against LCB.[134]

The various law enforcement and regulatory actions involving Joumaa, LCB and Lebanese exchange houses described above also highlight how terrorist organizations have financially benefited from TBML schemes originating in the United States. As detailed in the National ML Risk Assessment, TBML is used to disguise the origin of criminal proceeds through trade-related financial transactions, and includes a variety of schemes that can involve moving illicit goods, falsifying trade documents, and misrepresenting trade-related financial transactions with the purpose of disguising the origin of criminal proceeds and integrating the funds into the international financial system. Ayman Joumaa and other individuals involved in the drug trafficking and money laundering scheme described above used LCB and various Lebanese exchanges houses to facilitate wire transfers in furtherance of TBML schemes originating in the United States [135] As noted above, Hizballah indirectly derived financial support from the criminal activities of the Joumaa network, and members of this network were known to be supporters of Hizballah.[136]

Risk Summary

Given the important role that U.S. domestic demand plays in the global drug market, drug trafficking as a source of funding for terrorist groups, including the Taliban, FARC and Hizballah, presents a residual risk for TF.

c. Additional Criminal Activity: Extortion, Fraud and Smuggling

Aside from narco-trafficking and KFR, terrorists and terrorist organizations also engage in criminal activities for financial benefit. While such broad criminal activity occurs on a global scale, DOJ prosecutions demonstrate a U.S. nexus in some instances, as approximately 17 percent of the TF-related prosecutions and cases surveyed involved smuggling or fraudulent activity being used to raise funds for a terrorist organization.[137] Specifically, a cross reference of BSA reporting linked to FBI CT investigations has demonstrated that some established terrorist groups, especially Hizballah, are more involved in

---

[132] *United States v. Lebanese Canadian Bank SAL et al.*, Case No. 1:11-cv-09186 (Complaint) (S.D.N.Y, December 2011).

[133] Department of Justice, Press Release, "Manhattan U.S. Attorney Announces $102 Million Settlement Of Civil Forfeiture And Money Laundering Claims Against Lebanese Canadian Bank," June 25, 2013.

[134] *See* FinCEN, *Notice of Finding That Kassem Rmeiti & Co. Is a Financial Institution of Primary Money Laundering Concern*, Notice of Finding, 78 Fed. Reg. 24593, April 25, 2013; *see also* FinCEN, *Notice of Finding That Halawi Exchange Co. Is a Financial Institution of Primary Money Laundering Concern*, Notice of Finding, 78 Fed. Reg. 24596, April 25, 2013.

[135] FinCEN, *Finding That the Lebanese Canadian Bank SAL Is a Financial Institution of Primary Money Laundering Concern*, Notice of Finding, 76 Fed. Reg. 9403, February 17, 2011.

[136] *Id.*

[137] *See* Footnote 89.

criminal activity in the United States than other groups.[138] For example, Hizballah supporters in the United States historically used interstate cigarette smuggling to generate revenue that they then provided to Hizballah.[139] These cases involved the highly profitable but illegal business of smuggling cigarettes across state lines, from a state with a low cigarette tax to a state with a high cigarette tax.[140] Also, U.S. law enforcement has observed that as some terrorist groups find success with a criminal scheme, other groups will copy that scheme and use it for fund-raising purposes.

Terrorists and terrorist organizations may also use legitimate commercial enterprises in the United States to raise funds. Several law enforcement investigations and prosecutions have found a nexus between a commercial enterprise, including used car dealerships and restaurant franchises, and terrorist organizations, where revenue by the commercial enterprise was being routed to support a terrorist organization. However, given that these criminal cases are based around criminal conduct not involving terrorist organizations, such as bank or tax fraud, the connection to the terrorist organization may not be disclosed in the public charging documents.

The following case provides an example of smuggling being used to provide financial support to a terrorist organization, specifically Hizballah, and demonstrates how criminal activity can be a lucrative source of TF. In February 2010, U.S. authorities indicted four men and three businesses on charges relating to the export of hundreds of thousands of dollars' worth of electronics to Hizballah. The four men were indicted on charges for conspiring to smuggle goods to an import-export business located in the Galeria Page mall in Ciudad de Este, Paraguay.[141] Galeria Page serves as a source of fundraising for Hizballah and is locally considered to be the central headquarters for Hizballah members in the tri-border area between Paraguay, Brazil, and Argentina.[142] As such, the mall and all businesses inside were designated as SDGTs in 2006.[143] Three of the defendants were owners of freight-forwarding companies based in Florida and a fourth man owned the import-export business in Paraguay. One defendant used wire transfers to move funds to a bank in New Jersey from which he could pay for orders of videogame consoles. These wire transfer payments were routed through various financial institutions in order to mask their true origin. The three other defendants attempted to export the video game consoles by concealing the contents and destination of the shipments through falsified documents.[144]

Although less prevalent, fraud has also been used in the United States as a way to raise funds in support of terrorist organizations. In 2007 and 2008, for example, Khalid Ouazzani, a Moroccan-born U.S.

---

[138] Information derived from an analysis of financial institution BSA reporting cross-referenced with law enforcement investigations.

[139] *See* Michael Taxay, United States Attorneys' Bulletin, Vol. 62, No.5 (September 2014), "Terrorist Financing: Trends in the Prosecution of Terrorist Financing and Facilitation." Available at http://www.justice.gov/usao/eousa/foia_reading_room/usab6205.pdf. A recent review of law enforcement investigations and cases found that Hizballah no longer employs interstate cigarette smuggling in the United States as a major fundraising tool.

[140] *See, e.g, United States v. Hammoud*, 381 F.3d 316, 331–34 (4th Cir. 2004) (conviction for providing material support or resources to Hizballah).

[141] *See United States v. Mehdi et al.*, Case No. 1:09-cr-20852-ASG-3,5,7 (Indictment) (S.D. Fla. October 2009).

[142] Department of the Treasury, Press Release, "Treasury Targets Hizballah Fundraising Network in the Triple Frontier of Argentina, Brazil, and Paraguay," December 6, 2006.

[143] *Id.*

[144] *See United States v. Mehdi et al.*, Case No. 1:09-cr-20852-ASG-3,5,7 (Indictment) (S.D. Fla. October 2009).

citizen living in Kansas City, Missouri, provided more than $23,000 to AQ that were the proceeds of fraudulent activities.[145] Similarly, although extortion is a TF tactic that is more prevalent internationally than within the United States, it has been used against U.S. individuals and entities as well. Notably, in 2007, a U.S. corporation pleaded guilty to engaging in unlicensed transactions with a SDGT and paid a criminal fine of $25 million.[146] The plea agreement arose from millions of dollars' worth of payments that were made for years to the United Self-Defense Forces of Colombia to avoid harm to personnel and property. These payments were made by check and cash. Payments were directed by complicit corporate executives and continued even after attention had been called to the illegal activity by outside counsel.[147]

As described in the examples above, U.S. law enforcement and the DOJ have brought criminal cases under a variety of statutes where the proceeds of criminal activity are used to fund the activities of a terrorist organization.[148] In addition to criminal prosecutions and civil charges, the DOJ has also used asset forfeiture laws to seize and forfeit significant assets that would otherwise be used to provide support to terrorist organizations. For example, one forfeiture provision, Section 981(a)(1)(G), allows for both criminal and civil forfeiture of all assets related to terrorism.[149] Indeed, this forfeiture provision expressly enables law enforcement to seize and forfeit *all* assets, *wherever* located, of *anyone* engaged in planning or perpetrating acts of terrorism—regardless of whether the property was involved in the terrorist activity or is otherwise traceable to that activity, as required by most other forfeiture statutes.[150] Another forfeiture provision allows for the forfeiture of funds traceable to other offenses, including violations of IEEPA and AML laws.[151] A third provision provides for the forfeiture of property involved in money laundering.[152] A fourth provision allows for the forfeiture of funds in correspondent accounts to serve as a substitute for forfeitable funds held abroad.[153] These statutes have been used against a variety of entities that have facilitated TF, including against LCB and U.S.-based entities controlled by the Government of Iran.[154]

Risk Summary

As the statistics and cases presented in this section indicate, terrorists and their facilitators use a variety of criminal activities as a means of raising funds. Although smaller scale criminal activity such as fraud is certainly used to raise money, the instances of larger international criminal activity such as drug trafficking pose a risk because of the significant sum of funds involved. For these reasons, KFR poses a

---

[145] *See United States v. Khaled Ouazzani*, Case No. 10-00025-01-CR-W-HFS (Indictment) (W.D. Mo. February 2010). Ouazzani pled guilty to bank fraud for submitting false financial information to obtain a business loan, the proceeds of which were later provided for the use and benefit of AQ. Other TF cases have involved the use of tax and credit card fraud.

[146] Department of Justice, Press Release, "Chiquita Brands International Pleads Guilty to Making Payments to a Designated Terrorist Organization And Agrees to Pay $25 Million Fine," March 19, 2007.

[147] *Id.; see also United States v. Chiquita Brands Int'l, Inc.*, Case No. 1:07-cr-00055 (D.D.C. March 19, 2007).

[148] *See* Sharon Cohen Levin and Carolina A. Fornos, United States Attorneys' Bulletin, Vol. 62, No.5 (September 2014), "Using Criminal and Civil Forfeiture to Combat Terrorism and Terrorist Financing," (citing cases).

[149] *See* 18 U.S.C. § 981(a)(1)(G).

[150] Sharon Cohen Levin and Carolina A. Fornos, United States Attorneys Bulletin, Vol. 62, No.5 (September 2014), "Using Criminal and Civil Forfeiture to Combat Terrorism and Terrorist Financing."

[151] *See* 18 U.S.C. § 981(a)(1)(C).

[152] *See id.* § 981(a)(1)(A).

[153] *See id.* § 981(k). In order to transact in U.S. dollars, most foreign banks maintain accounts at U.S. banks. Such accounts are called "correspondent accounts."

[154] *See* Michael Taxay, United States Attorneys Bulletin, Vol. 62, No.5 (September 2014), "Terrorist Financing: Trends in the Prosecution of Terrorist Financing and Facilitation."

significant global TF risk. Additionally, the criminal activity is not limited to a single group or a single type of crime. As the cases demonstrate, numerous terrorist groups can be implicated in the same drug trafficking activity and, as Hizballah demonstrates, a single group can be involved in numerous types of criminal activity. Although much of this activity occurs globally, the cases in which U.S. persons are implicated demonstrate that this activity poses a TF risk to the United States as well. This TF risk is likely to persist as terrorists continue to rely on criminal activity for sources of financing, especially if other sources of TF are successfully combated.

2. MISUSE OF CHARITABLE[155] ORGANIZATIONS AND INDIVIDUALS RAISING FUNDS UNDER THE AUSPICES OF CHARITABLE GIVING

Globally, terrorist groups and their supporters continue to take advantage of charitable organizations and charitable giving to exploit donations and operations to support terrorist activities. The abuse of Non-profit Organizations (NPOs) to facilitate TF is an area of focus for the FATF, the G-7, and the UN, as well as national authorities in many regions, including the United States. As called for in the FATF international standards, the United States assesses, monitors, and takes necessary actions to protect the large, diverse U.S. charitable sector and charitably minded donors from terrorist abuse on an ongoing basis using a risk-based approach. As will be described in more detail below, the United States engages a wide variety of agencies and authorities to promote effective supervision of the relevant sections of the charitable sector that are most at risk as well as to obtain information about specific threats to the sector and consider appropriate actions to take. New information related to specific cases and analyses of trends are reviewed by relevant government authorities on an ongoing basis to work towards preventing TF and taking action when such abuse is identified.

a. Charitable Organizations

FATF defines NPOs to be "a legal person or arrangement or organization that primarily engages in raising or disbursing funds for purposes such as charitable, religious, cultural, educational, social or fraternal purposes, or for the carrying out of other types of "good works." In the United States, to facilitate fundraising, these types of NPOs falling within the FATF definition generally apply for tax-exempt status with the IRS, which permits their donors to deduct funds donated on their income tax returns, and are regulated as "tax-exempt charitable organizations"[156] by the IRS, which generally includes the annual filing of required forms and disclosures. Some organizations, such as houses of worship, are not required to apply for exempt status with the IRS or file annual information reports, but they may need to register and make annual filings with state authorities to comply with state and/or local fundraising requirements. Other organizations, such as taxable non-profit organizations or for-profit organizations, may raise funds

---

[155] The term "charitable" as used herein is intended in its broadest sense, to include charitable, humanitarian, religious, educational, and other organizations and philanthropic individuals, and unless otherwise indicated, is not limited to organizations that the IRS has determined are tax-exempt charitable organizations under Section 501(c)(3) of the IRC.

[156] Qualified tax-exempt organizations obtain their tax-exempt status under Section 501(c)(3) of the IRC. Such organizations are religious, educational, charitable, scientific, or literary organizations; testing for public safety organizations; and organizations preventing cruelty to children or animals, or fostering national or international amateur sports competition. The IRC provides tax-exemption for certain non-charitable organizations, such as social welfare organizations under Section 501(c)(4) and business leagues under 501(c)(6).

without applying for tax-exempt status, but like all institutions they must file tax returns with the IRS, regardless of their taxable status.

The IRS, which administers federal tax laws and regulations related to tax-exempt charitable organizations, looks to various organizational factors and the structure of an organization to determine the level of TF risk posed, including the activities, domestic and cross-border, conducted by the tax exempt organization, its mission statement and filings, financial transactions such as assets held by the tax-exempt organization, donations and expenditures.

i.   Nature of the TF Vulnerability of Charitable Organizations

Based on a review of publicly-available information on U.S. law enforcement cases involving terrorism and TF offenses, information obtained from financial institution reporting and Treasury designations of charitable organizations for financing terrorist organizations,[157] some charitable organizations, particularly those based or operating in high-risk jurisdictions, continue to be vulnerable to abuse for TF. An analysis of the TF-related investigations and prosecutions surveyed for this assessment found that fundraising through charitable organizations accounted for about 20 percent of the overall observed methods of fundraising for terrorist organizations.[158] As of December 31, 2014, Treasury has designated 54 charities, along with some additional branches and associated individuals, for their support to terrorist organizations under Executive Order (E.O.) 13224.[159] Out of these global designations, the United States has designated eight charities with operations in the United States.[160] Also, U.S. financial intelligence derived from the analysis of financial institution reporting filed with FinCEN demonstrates the potential abuse of charitable organizations globally by terrorists, terrorist organizations, and those associated with or supporting them to raise, move, and place funds in the U.S. financial system.[161] Since 2003, there have been an increasing number of SARs filed that include charitable organizations as the subject, with more than 5,000 SARs filed in 2013.[162]

The extent of the TF risk for charitable organizations in the United States varies dramatically depending on the operations and activities of the charitable organization. For example, there are approximately one million charitable organizations[163] in the United States that have been determined by the IRS to be eligible for tax-exempt status, the vast majority of which pose little or no TF risk. However, for those

---

[157] A list of charitable organizations designated by Treasury is available at http://www.treasury.gov/resource-center/terrorist-illicit-finance/Pages/protecting-fto.aspx.

[158] *See* Footnote 89.

[159] *See* OFAC, *2014 Terrorist Assets Report*. In total, as of December 31, 2014 there are 894 individuals and entities designated under E.O. 13224 that remain on the Specially Designated Nationals and Blocked Persons (SDN) list for being owned or controlled by, acting for or on behalf of, or providing support or services to a SDGT, usually also a designated FTO.

[160] *See* Department of the Treasury, Resource Center, "Designated Charities and Potential Fundraising Front Organizations for FTOs." Available at http://www.treasury.gov/resource-center/terrorist-illicit-finance/Pages/protecting-fto.aspx.

[161] Information derived from an analysis of financial institution BSA reporting.

[162] *Id.*

[163] Of approximately 1.6 million entities that the IRS has determined are eligible for tax-exempt status, approximately one million are "charitable organizations." *See* IRS Pub. 55B, *Data Book* (2013), Table 25 at p. 56. Available at http://www.irs.gov/pub/irs-soi/13databk.pdf. This does not count charitable organizations, like houses of worship, which are not required to apply for tax-exemption or file annual information returns.

charitable organizations with U.S. tax exemption operating abroad or with overseas branches, particularly in high-risk areas where terrorist groups are most active, such as Pakistan, Somalia and Syria, the risks can be significant, highlighting the importance of accountability of charitable funding. Terrorist groups and their supporters continue to take advantage of charitable organizations to infiltrate the charitable sector and exploit donations and operations to support terrorist activities.

Terrorist groups and their supporters may seek to exploit charities and charitable giving for a number of reasons. Charities can be established or otherwise used to provide a veil of legitimacy needed to cover the movement of funds, personnel, military supplies, and other resources by terrorist groups and their associates, including to high-risk areas where they operate.

There have been many examples around the world of charities that have been integral components of terrorist networks. Examples include: the Revival of the Islamic Heritage Society (RIHS), which Treasury designated for providing financial and material support to the AQ network; FIF, which Treasury designated for providing financial support to LT; the Al-Waqfiya Al-Ri'aya Al-Usra Al-Filistinya Wa Al-Lubnanya, which Treasury designated for providing financial support to Hamas; and the Iranian Committee for the Reconstruction of Lebanon, which Treasury designated for providing financial, material and technical support to Hizballah.[164]

Terrorist exploitation of charities and charitable giving has not been limited to organizations located overseas. There have been several examples of terrorist groups and their support networks raising funds through charities in the United States as well. For example, Treasury designated the Tamils Rehabilitation Organization (TRO) on November 15, 2007 for serving as a front to facilitate fundraising and procurement for the designated terrorist group Liberation Tigers of Tamil Eelam (LTTE).[165] In the United States, TRO raised funds on behalf of the LTTE through a network of individual representatives. TRO also facilitated LTTE procurement operations in the United States, including the purchase of munitions, equipment, communication devices, and other technology for the LTTE. TRO's efforts worldwide reportedly allowed the LTTE to use humanitarian aid, which TRO collected from the international community after the December 2004 tsunami, to launch new campaigns to strengthen LTTE's military capacity.[166] In addition to the Treasury designations, a number of TRO affiliated criminal prosecutions also took place between 2006 and 2009.[167] Most notably, the director of the American branch of the TRO, who pleaded guilty to conspiring to provide material support to a terrorist

---

[164] Department of the Treasury, Resource Center, "Protecting Charitable Giving: Frequently Asked Questions," June 4, 2010. Available at http://www.treasury.gov/resource-center/terrorist-illicit-finance/Documents/Treasury%20Charity%20FAQs%206-4-2010%20FINAL.pdf.

[165] Department of the Treasury, Press Release, "Treasury Targets Charity Covertly Supporting Violence in Sri Lanka, November 15, 2007.

[166] *Id.*

[167] Indictment documents charged over 10 defendants with a range of legal violations including conspiracy to provide material support to a designated FTO [LTTE], conspiracy to bribe a public official, attempt to obtain classified material, violations of the International Emergency Economic Powers Act (IEEPA), conspiracy to export prohibited arms and munitions, attempt to export prohibited arms and munitions, international money laundering and possession of arms in the commission of a felony. *See, e.g., United States v. Thavaraja*, 740 F.3d 253, 254 (2d Cir. 2014).

organization, oversaw and directed the LTTE's various activities in the United States , including raising millions of dollars for the LTTE and laundering it through the TRO.[168]

Evidence suggests that terrorists and their support networks are aware of the ways in which charitable organizations can be abused as a cover to raise, move, and use funds and actively seek to exploit them. In a recent investigation, one defendant noted to a confidential informant that he "was involving himself in a non-profit from which he could build resources and money which he could then siphon away and provide to the brothers fighting in Afghanistan," adding that "the reason for the use of a non-profit is because when he has attempted [to] send money by other means he has immediately been questioned as to where the money is going."[169]

While some terrorist supporters create sham charities as a cover to raise and move funds, other terrorist groups and their supporters use charities to provide funds or otherwise dispense critical social or humanitarian services to vulnerable populations in an effort to radicalize communities and build local support. Charities established or controlled by terrorist groups and persons assisting their causes can help fund the operation of schools, religious institutions, and hospitals that may create fertile recruitment grounds or generate dependency among vulnerable populations for these essential services. For example, from 1993 through 2001, the Holy Land Foundation for Relief and Development (HLF) operated as the chief U.S. fundraising arm of Hamas. As noted by one U.S. court, "[t]he financial link between the Holy Land Foundation and Hamas was established at the foundation's genesis and continued until it was severed by the Government's intervention in 2001."[170] U.S. prosecutors demonstrated at trial that HLF intentionally cloaked its financial support for Hamas by funneling money through Zakat Committees and Charitable Societies in the West Bank and Gaza.[171] In some cases, the defendants targeted financial aid specifically for families related to well-known Hamas operatives who had been killed or jailed. In this manner, the defendants effectively rewarded past and encouraged future terrorist activities. After a jury trial, HLF's principals were convicted of providing material support to a FTO, as well as tax and money laundering violations, and received substantial terms of imprisonment (the longest being 65 years), and the organization was ordered to forfeit over $12 million.[172]

      ii.   U.S. Government Efforts to Mitigate Vulnerabilities Against TF Abuse of Charitable Organizations

Recognizing the past TF threats and vulnerabilities associated with abuse of the charitable organizations, the U.S. government has taken enforcement actions when appropriate against both charitable organizations and individuals, strengthened oversight and internal coordination, and conducted sustained outreach to the charitable sector and donor communities to raise awareness of the vulnerability and provide guidance on risk mitigation best practices.

---

[168] *See* Department of Justice, Press Release, "Four Plead Guilty To Conspiring To Provide Material Support To The LTTE, A Foreign Terrorist Organization," June 9, 2009.
[169] *New York v. Humayoun Ghoulam Nabi and Ismail Alsarabbi*, Q13800646, Q13800647 (Complaint) (N.Y. Crim. Ct. October 10, 2013).
[170] *United States v. El Mezain*, 664 F.3d 467, 484 (5th Cir. 2011).
[171] *See* Michael Taxay, United States Attorneys' Bulletin, Vol. 62, No.5, (September 2014), "Terrorist Financing: Trends in the Prosecution of Terrorist Financing and Facilitation."
[172] *Id.*

Criminal and Civil Prosecutions

In the aftermath of the September 11, 2001 terrorist attacks, the DOJ has investigated, prosecuted and convicted several large charities and/or their principals, including the Benevolence International Foundation , HLF, the Islamic American Relief Agency (self-described as the U.S. affiliate of the Islamic African Relief Agency), the Child Foundation, TRO, and Care International.[173] These organizations were convicted of violations of multiple statutes criminalizing TF, including providing material support to a FTO and violations of U.S. economic sanctions.[174]

In addition to prosecuting charitable organizations under statutes criminalizing TF, the DOJ and other LEAs can also utilize authorities under the IRC to impose additional criminal and civil liability on tax-exempt charitable and taxable organizations that provide support to terrorist organizations. For example, DOJ's Tax Division, which provides assistance in TF cases involving criminal violations of the IRC, may prosecute entities that conceal their affiliation with a terrorist organization, either an FTO or SDGT, or their affiliation with a foreign entity connected to an FTO or SDGT, through the filing of false tax forms with the IRS.[175] Likewise, the IRS may revoke the tax-exempt status of an organization, including one affiliated with terrorism, that omitted or misstated a material fact or operated in a manner materially different from that originally represented.[176] In that situation, a charity would lose its coveted tax-exempt status, and its financial affiliations with terrorist organizations may be exposed. Also, the IRS publicly suspends the tax-exempt status of any organization designated as an FTO, Specially Designated Terrorist (SDT), or SDGT.[177] This loss and exposure probably would cause its donor base to shrink, depriving the affiliated terrorist organization of a key source of funding.[178]

A 2011 U.S. Court of Appeals decision upholding the conviction of three officers of Care International for several criminal violations of the IRC, including willfully filing false tax returns, demonstrates the potential effectiveness of this type of criminal prosecution.[179] In particular, the court noted that Care International's failure to disclose its publication of the pro-jihad newsletter, "Al-Hussam," and its financial support of orphans, which was in support of the children of deceased terrorists, was sufficient to justify a conviction for intentionally failing to disclose activities that were not previously reported to the IRS on earlier tax returns or Care International's tax exempt application.[180] The use of this particular strategy to investigate and prosecute tax-exempt charitable organizations alleged to be involved in TF is made by the relevant law enforcement agencies and DOJ on a case-by-case basis.

---

[173] *Id.*

[174] *See e.g., United States v. El Mezain,* 664 F.3d at 484 ; *See United States v. Islamic African Relief Agency,* No. 07-00087-01/07-CR-W-NKL at *15 (Second Superseding Indictment) (W.D. Mo. 2007).

[175] *See e.g., United States v. Mubayyid,* 658 F.3d 35 (1st Cir. 2011).

[176] *See* 26 C.F.R. § 601.201(n)(6)(i).

[177] *See* 26 U.S.C. § 501(p).

[178] *See* Corey J. Smith, United States Attorneys' Bulletin, Vol. 6, No. 3 (May 2013), *Tax Enforcement II*, "Terrorism Tax Evasion: Using Criminal Tax Charges to Combat the Use of Charities in Terrorism Financing."

[179] *See United States v. Mubayyid,* 658 F.3d 35 (1st Cir. 2011).

[180] *See* Corey J. Smith, United States Attorneys' Bulletin, Vol. 6, No. 3 (May 2013), *Tax Enforcement II*, "Terrorism Tax Evasion: Using Criminal Tax Charges to Combat the Use of Charities in Terrorism Financing" (citing *United States v. Mubayyid,* 658 F.3d 35 (1st Cir. 2011).

NPO Reporting Requirements

In addition, the IRS as the U.S. tax regulator has increased reporting requirements for some tax-exempt organizations in order to enhance transparency and mitigate TF risk within the charitable sector. Any U.S.-based charitable organization that wants to maintain its status as a tax-exempt entity under IRC section 501(c)(3), including foreign charitable organizations desiring tax-exempt status in the United States, must make annual information filings with the IRS.[181] The IRS redesigned Form 990 in 2008 to include more information regarding tax exempt organizations' stated mission, programs and finances, including a wide range of information about donors, activities and funds sent and used abroad that are required on Schedule F of Form 990.[182] The redesigned form includes (1) a checklist to show which schedules the filing organization must complete, thereby simplifying the core form, (2) provides more opportunity throughout the form for supplemental information, (3) contains revised governance and compensation sections, and (4) has modified other areas of the form, including non-cash contributions and supplemental financial information.

Monitoring of financial reports for transparency and accountability by the IRS may lead to further investigations that provide more insight into potential underlying illicit actions, including TF. IRS-TE/GE examines tax-exempt organizations for compliance with the U.S. tax laws, including reviewing the reporting forms, and IRS-CI conducts criminal investigations, as they become necessary. Within IRS-TE/GE is also a financial investigations unit composed of forensic investigators and specialists with specific financial expertise to pursue cases of potential misuse of charities for a range of purposes, ranging from fraud and tax evasion to illicit finance.[183] More complex illicit finance cases are handled in cooperation with other relevant U.S. government agencies and offices.

Outreach to the Charitable Sector

In addition to better annual reporting and continued enforcement actions when terrorist threats have been identified within the charitable sector, the federal government continues to engage in direct outreach to the charitable sector and donor communities by raising awareness of the risk of terrorist abuse of charitable organizations and providing guidance on risk mitigation best practices and efforts to protect the sector from terrorist abuse. As part of this effort, Treasury provides guidance for charities and donors to help protect themselves against such TF abuse and has published a number of resource documents for the sector, including a risk matrix, voluntary charitable guidelines and best practices, frequently asked questions, and specific guidance regarding certain sanctions programs and/or global developments, such as sending humanitarian assistance to Somalia, Syria and Iran.[184] In October 2014 OFAC issued

---

[181] See IRS, *Compliance Guide for Public 501(c)3 Charities*. Available at http://www.irs.gov/pub/irs-pdf/p4221pc.pdf.

[182] See IRS, Chronological History: Redesign of the 2008 Form 990 and Corresponding Instructions. Available at http://www.irs.gov/Charities-&-Non-Profits/Charitable-Organizations/Chronological-History:-Redesign-of-the-2008-Form-990-and-Corresponding-Instructions.

[183] Any matter criminal in nature, as stated above (to include tax evasion, illicit finance and fraud) is investigated by IRS-CI with technical assistance provided by IRS's TE/GE financial investigations unit. For criminal investigations, TE/GE's financial investigations unit renders technical assistance to IRS-CI on accounting, tax law, and procedural issues regarding charities and other NPOs.

[184] See Department of the Treasury, Resource Center, "Protecting Charitable Organizations."

humanitarian guidance for charities and donors working in a variety of high risk environments in which sanctions are in place.[185]

The governmental and charitable sector share the same goal of protecting and promoting safe charitable giving. Recognizing this shared goal and the vulnerability faced by the sector to terrorist abuse, many charitable organizations have also strengthened their internal controls and procedures over the years, including through the use of Treasury's voluntary charitable guidelines.[186] There have been greater self-regulation initiatives within the sector to help promote greater transparency and accountability of funding and operations, including screening public terrorist lists and having more robust due diligence measures in place to help protect against diversion of funds and essential services that may be used to support terrorist organizations.[187] Some charitable organizations operating overseas have developed sophisticated internal controls and procedures, including end use monitoring systems, in an effort to prevent misuse of funding and services. In addition to U.S. government enforcement action, reporting requirements and outreach efforts described above, these measures help mitigate TF risk in the sector.

Risk Summary

Through a combination of targeted enforcement action, focused oversight, sustained outreach, and extensive international engagement and cooperation to address global terrorist threats in the charitable sector, the U.S. government, working with the charitable sector, has reduced the opportunity for U.S. charitable organizations to be abused to facilitate financial support for terrorist groups. However, given the large size and diversity of the U.S. charitable sector and its global reach, the sector remains vulnerable to abuse.

    b.   Individuals Fund Raising Under the Auspices of Charitable Giving

At the same time, based on financial institution reporting and a review of publicly-available information on U.S. law enforcement cases involving TF, the United States has seen an increase in fundraising under the auspices of charitable giving, particularly by individual fundraisers, without the use of specific charitable organizations. In the survey of law enforcement cases mentioned above, the second largest grouping of cases, approximately 24 percent, involved individuals raising proceeds on behalf of humanitarian causes without a link to an established charitable organization.[188] This method of soliciting donations has also taken on an increasing importance for terrorist groups. Of the cases examined, only

---

[185] *See* OFAC, *Guidance Related to the Provision of Humanitarian Assistance by Not-for-Profit Non-Governmental Organizations*, October 17, 2014. In the case of targeted financial sanctions administered by OFAC, in certain instances, OFAC may use its authority to license transactions that otherwise would be prohibited, when doing so would further U.S. foreign policy. OFAC regularly promulgates in its regulations what are known as "general licenses" authorizing certain categories of otherwise prohibited activity for all those who meet its terms, and it also grants specific licenses on a case-by-case basis. For additional information regarding the applicability of targeted financial sanctions to charitable organizations, *see* Department of the Treasury, Protecting Charitable Giving: Frequently Asked Questions, June 4, 2010.

[186] *See* Department of the Treasury, *Anti-Terrorist Financing Guidelines: Voluntary Best Practices for U.S.-based Charities*, September 2009. Available at http://www.treasury.gov/resource-center/terrorist-illicit-finance/Documents/guidelines_charities.pdf.

[187] *See* FATF, Risk of Terrorist Abuse in Non-Profit Organisations, June 2014.

[188] *See* Footnote 89.

four cases prior to 2006 involved such fundraising, while there have been 14 cases involving this type of activity since then.

In several of the cases examined, terrorist financiers acting as individual fundraisers preyed on unwitting donors' good intentions and at times specifically targeted certain diaspora communities. These terrorist facilitators seek to avoid the oversight and reporting necessary for formal charitable organizations and instead solicit funds under the auspices of charity, but are unaffiliated with any charitable organization recognized by the U.S. government, then divert the proceeds to fund terrorist activity.

U.S. law enforcement has responded to these emerging trends through a nationally coordinated campaign of investigations and criminal prosecutions that target this specific TF method. For example, the FBI initiated Operation Green Arrow to stem the flow of money from the United States to Al-Shabaab and other insurgents in Somalia.[189] These individuals used a variety of methods to raise funds for Al-Shabaab, including door-to-door personal solicitations and teleconferences.[190] Although the amount raised by these individuals was not substantial compared to other TF cases (each sent approximately $16,000 to Somalia), it was considered an important revenue source by Al-Shabaab's leadership, which routinely directly communicated with the fundraisers.[191] In one case, two naturalized U.S. citizens of Somali origin were sentenced for providing material support to Al-Shabaab. They solicited funds in person in Somali communities in the United States and Canada under the false pretense that the funds were for the poor and needy, but the donations went to support Al-Shabaab. The individuals also participated in teleconferences that featured speakers who encouraged donations to support Al-Shabaab.[192]

Following the success of Operation Green Arrow, the FBI initiated Operation Rhino, which responded to the threat posed by persons traveling from the United States to join Al-Shabaab in Somalia.[193] The U.S. government identified an increase in individuals who had traveled from the United States to engage in violent jihad overseas, which was particularly troubling due to concern that these "travelers" will return to the United States battle-hardened and fully indoctrinated in violent jihad and more likely to engage in domestic terrorist activity.[194] These travelers require facilitators, which increasingly goes hand-in-hand with financing. Operation Rhino resulted in charges against more than 20 travelers and facilitators and nine convictions to date, including facilitators who provided funds to pay for travel and weapons in Somalia.[195] One defendant convicted for providing material support to Al-Shabaab admitted that he helped raise funds for Al-Shabaab from the Somali-American community in Minnesota under false pretenses, claiming the money raised would be used for a local mosque or to help orphans in Somalia, when, in fact, it was for purchasing airline tickets and paying other expenses for men who traveled from

---

[189] *See* Michael Taxay, United States Attorneys' Bulletin, Vol. 62, No.5 (September 2014), "Terrorist Financing: Trends in the Prosecution of Terrorist Financing and Facilitation."

[190] *Id.*

[191] *Id.*

[192] *See United States v. Ali et al.*, Case No. 0:10-cr-00187 (Sentencing Memorandum) (D. Minn, April 2013).

[193] *See* Michael Taxay, United States Attorneys' Bulletin, Vol. 62, No.5 (September 2014), "Terrorist Financing: Trends in the Prosecution of Terrorist Financing and Facilitation."

[194] *See Id.*

[195] *See Id.* (citing *United States v. Omar*, Case No. 09-CR-242-MJD/FLN (Report and Recommendation) (D. Minn. 2012); *United States v. Mohamed*, 09-CR-352-MJD/FLN (Government's Trial Brief) (D. Minn. 2011).

Minneapolis to Somalia to join Al-Shabaab.[196]   In a separate Al-Shabaab-related case, the defendant purportedly described at a gathering of co-conspirators his own plans to fight "jihad" against Ethiopians, and he raised money to buy airplane tickets for others to make the trip to Somalia for the same purpose.[197] In raising that money, however, he allegedly misled community members into thinking they were contributing money to send young men to Saudi Arabia to study the Koran.[198]

Another method found in U.S. prosecutions for providing material support for terrorism is the increasing use of the internet and social media to solicit donations that are often provided to terrorist organizations or their supporters. In the TF-related cases and prosecutions reviewed, online fundraising was involved in nine cases; in all but two of those cases, the criminal activity began after 2007.[199] The ability to easily reach potential donors and connect with like-minded supporters helps to raise and move funds quickly, less transparently, and often for illicit purposes. Of the TF cases examined, nine were identified as including personal fundraising online or through social media, as opposed to soliciting donations through a formal, established organization. A FinCEN analysis of financial institution reporting showed individuals with alleged links to AQ, the Taliban, Hamas, and Chechen Mujahideen using personal PayPal accounts to collect funds for named causes.[200] Several Treasury designations of terrorist supporters have also cited the use of social media to solicit funds.[201] The Syrian conflict has seen a significant use of the internet and social media sites, such as Twitter and Facebook, to solicit sizable donations that include support to designated terrorist organizations and their supporters. A number of online fundraisers explicitly advertise that collected funds are being used to purchase weapons and other equipment for extremist groups and post videos and photos verifying the receipt of donations by fighters. One Kuwait-based campaign claimed to have raised enough cash to arm 12,000 fighters.[202]

Risk Summary

There has been a shift in recent years towards individuals with no connections to a charitable organization recognized by the U.S. government soliciting funds under the auspices of charity for a variety of terrorist groups, including AQ, Al-Shabaab, Hamas, ISIL, and the Taliban, often online and using personal accounts or informal channels. This shift probably is due in part to the comprehensive, multi-faceted approach to preventing TF abuse of tax exempt charitable organizations, including U.S. government oversight, enforcement actions, outreach to and engagement with the charitable sector, and international cooperation. This trend highlights the need for continued outreach to the charitable sector and donor community on the evolving TF threats and vulnerabilities the sector faces combined with continued use of

---

[196] *See United States v. Ahmed Hussain Mahamud*, Case No. CR-11-191-DWF/AJB (Plea Agreement and Sentencing Stipulations) (D. Minn. 2012). The defendant sent money via wire transfers to a co-conspirator in Somalia, knowing the money would be used to purchase weapons or otherwise support Al-Shabaab.

[197] *United States v. Isse et al.*, Case No. 0:09-cr-00050 (Third Superseding Indictment) (D. Minn. July 2010); *see also* Department of Justice, Press Release "Fourteen Charged with Providing Material Support to Somalia-Based Terrorist Organization Al-Shabaab," August 5, 2010.

[198] *Id.*

[199] *See* Footnote 89.

[200] Information derived from an analysis of financial institution BSA reporting.

[201] *See* Department of the Treasury, Press Release, "Treasury Designates Three Key Supporters of Terrorists in Syria and Iraq," August 6, 2014.

[202] *See* Elizabeth Dickinson, *Playing with Fire: Why Private Gulf Financing for Syria's Extremist Rebels Risks Igniting Sectarian Conflict at Home*, p. 13, December 6, 2013 (Brookings Institution).

existing government authorities to investigate, prosecute, or sanction those individuals abusing charitable organizations or charitable giving for TF.

3. *INDIVIDUAL CONTRIBUTIONS/SELF-FUNDING*

In addition to raising funds through charitable organizations or causes, as described above, terrorist groups also benefit from funds provided directly by U.S. citizens. An analysis of TF-related law enforcement cases and prosecutions since 2001 found that direct financial support from individuals to terrorist networks occurred in approximately 33 percent of the cases reviewed.[203] In these cases, U.S. citizens or residents were observed soliciting funds to support their own planned terrorist activity, including paying for their travels and living expenses to fight alongside terrorist groups overseas. In 2006, a U.S. citizen, Kobie Williams, pleaded guilty to conspiring to train with firearms in preparation to join the Taliban as well as contributing several hundred dollars to the Taliban to further this effort.[204] Recently, another U.S. citizen, Michael Todd Wolfe, was indicted by a federal grand jury for attempting to provide material support to ISIL.[205] Wolfe allegedly planned to travel to the Middle East to provide his services to radical groups engaged in armed conflict in Syria, using an expected tax refund of $5,000 to cover his travel expenses. Of particular concern is that these homegrown violent extremists may use this type of activity to fund domestic terrorist activity in support of extremist ideology espoused by a terrorist group, but without direct assistance from the terrorist group.

U.S. authorities have also observed foreign persons directly soliciting U.S. residents for financial and non-cash contributions to terrorist groups, frequently using social media. For example, Babar Ahmad, a UK resident, established and operated a family of websites known as Azzam Publications to enable individuals, including U.S. residents, to contribute directly to terrorist groups.[206] Through those sites, which espoused the rhetoric of violent jihad, Ahmad solicited contributions from U.S. residents of funds, equipment, and personnel for a variety of terrorist groups, including the Taliban.[207] U.S. officials successfully extradited Ahmad from the UK, and he pleaded guilty in 2013 to conspiracy to provide and actually providing funds, physical items, and personnel to the Taliban.[208]

Although these cases tend to involve small amounts of money, they pose a domestic TF risk. U.S. law enforcement and regulatory authorities have aggressively sought to prevent this type of activity and take appropriate enforcement actions. As described above, the DOJ indicted Michael Todd Wolfe for providing material support to a FTO, in addition to other charges. The DOJ also indicted Mufid Elfgeeh for providing material support to ISIL, which included sending funds to foreign terrorist fighters who

---

[203] See Footnote 89.

[204] *See* Department of Justice, Press Release, "U.S. Citizen Taliban Supporter Sentenced to Prison," August 7, 2009.

[205] *See* FBI, Press Release, "Austinite Pleads Guilty to Attempting to Provide Material Support to Terrorists," June 27, 2014.

[206] *See* Michael Taxay, United States Attorneys Bulletin, Vol. 62, No.5 (September 2014), "Terrorist Financing: Trends in the Prosecution of Terrorist Financing and Facilitation."

[207] *See United States v. Ahmad*, No. 3:04M240-WIG (Affidavit in Support of Request for Extradition) (D. Conn. 2003).

[208] Department of Justice, Press Release, "Two British Nationals Plead Guilty To Terrorism-related Charges In New Haven Federal Court," December 10, 2013.

were attempting to travel to Syria to join and fight for ISIL.[209] These indictments, along with others mentioned above, highlight the important interaction between sanctions designations and criminal liability for TF, as designating an entity as an FTO permits law enforcement authorities to investigate and prosecute individuals for providing financial support to a designated entity, without having to additionally demonstrate direct support for terrorist activity by the individuals' or entities.[210]

To assist these law enforcement efforts, FinCEN has automated "business rules" to search BSA reporting daily for key terms, entities, or typologies of national security interest. The rules are designed to screen daily filings and identify reports that merit further review by analysts. For example, as of May 2015, rules related to ISIL alone generate more than eight hundred matches each month for further review and exploitation. FinCEN's analysis of this reporting has revealed new foreign terrorist fighters and their networks, furthering ongoing domestic and foreign law enforcement investigations.

Risk Summary

Nonetheless, despite the aggressive efforts of U.S. law enforcement authorities to combat such activity, given the small dollar value of such activity and the limited number of individuals involved, identification of such activity is particularly challenging. Additionally, these funds could be used to facilitate organized or "lone-wolf" style attacks by homegrown violent extremists or foreign terrorist fighters returning to the United States from Syria or Iraq. Therefore, individual donations made in the United States to terrorist groups or self-funding by U.S. citizens or residents poses a residual TF risk to the United States.

---

[209] Department of Justice, Press Release, "Rochester Man Indicted on Charges of Attempting to Provide Material Support to ISIS, Attempting to Kill U.S. Soldiers and Possession of Firearms and Silencers," September 16, 2014.
[210] For example, 18 U.S.C. § 2339B, the most frequently used TF criminal statute, prohibits persons from knowingly providing material support or resources to an FTO. This statute reflects recognition of the fact that terrorist organizations can have multiple wings, to include military, political, and social, and that material support to any of these wings ultimately supports the organization's violent activities.

B. MOVING AND PLACING FUNDS: VULNERABILITIES AND RISKS

The growth and increasing sophistication of the international financial system in recent years has enabled illicit actors to place and move money, hide assets, and conduct transactions anywhere in the world, exposing financial centers to exploitation and abuse in an unprecedented way. The United States has seen a wide variety of terrorist groups, including AQ and its affiliates, Al-Shabaab, Hamas and Hizballah, use banks[211] and MSBs[212] to place and transfer funds, along with cash transportation provided by cash couriers.[213]

The AML/CFT controls required by the U.S. regulatory framework aid financial institutions in identifying risk, provide valuable information to law enforcement, and inform U.S. national security policy. These required measures include the establishment of AML programs and reporting and record keeping requirements to provide useful information to law enforcement and national security authorities for the purpose of combating the full range of illicit finance threats. An AML program must include, at a minimum, a system of internal controls to ensure ongoing compliance, independent testing, designation of an individual responsible for managing BSA compliance and training for appropriate personnel.[214] An effective AML/CFT regime also includes enhanced due diligence procedures for those customers that present a high risk for money laundering or TF, as well as for the provision of foreign correspondent accounts and private banking services.[215] However, when these safeguards are not effectively implemented or stringently enforced, money launderers, terrorist financiers and other illicit actors are able to abuse the U.S. financial system.

The combination of a strong AML/CFT legal framework and effective supervision has succeeded in making it more difficult for terrorists and their facilitators to access the U.S. financial system, often forcing support networks to resort to costlier and/or riskier means of meeting their operational needs.[216] Terrorist groups have increasingly turned to unregulated channels, including unlicensed money

---

[211] Under the BSA, as implemented by 31 C.F.R. § 1010.100, the term "bank" includes each agent, agency, branch or office within the U.S. of commercial banks, savings and loan associations, thrift institutions, credit unions, and foreign banks. The term "bank" is used throughout this document generically to refer to these financial institutions.

[212] An MSB is defined under the implementing regulations for the BSA to be "any person doing business, whether or not on a regular basis or as an organized business concern, in one or more of the following capacities: (1) Currency dealer or exchanger; (2) Check casher; (3) Issuer of traveler's checks, money orders or stored value; (4) Seller or redeemer of traveler's checks, money orders or stored value; (5) Money transmitter; and (6) U.S. Postal Service." 31 C.F.R. § 1010.100(ff). However, banks and securities and commodities brokers that are regulated by the federal functional regulators are excluded from the definition of MSB. *Id.*

[213] For example, banks and MSBs accounted for over 90 percent of all financial institution SAR filings with the subject line "terrorist financing." *See* FinCEN, SAR Stats. Available at http://www.fincen.gov/Reports/SARStats.

[214] *See, e.g.,* 12 C.F.R. § 21.21 (national banks); 12 C.F.R. § 208.61 (state member banks); 12 C.F.R. § 326.8 (non-member banks); 12 C.F.R. § 748.2 (credit unions); FINRA Rule 3310 (securities broker-dealers); and National Futures Association Rule 2-9(c) (commodities brokers and futures commission merchants). *See also* Federal Financial Institutions Examination Council (FFIEC) BSA/AML Examination Manual (2014), pp. 28-29. Available at https://www.ffiec.gov/bsa_aml_infobase/documents/BSA_AML_Man_2014.pdf.

[215] *See id.* at 112-118 & 125-129. *See also Joint Guidance on Obtaining and Retaining Beneficial Ownership Information,* FIN– 2010–G001, March 5, 2010.

[216] *See* David Cohen, Under Secretary for Terrorism and Financial Intelligence, Department of the Treasury, Remarks before the Center for a New American Security, "Confronting New Threats in Terrorist Financing,'" March 4, 2014.

transmitters and cash couriers, to transfer and move funds. However, the capacity of banks to quickly facilitate large cross border transactions makes them a target for abuse by illicit actors.

Broadly speaking, based on an analysis of U.S. law enforcement investigations and prosecutions relating to TF, two methods of moving money to terrorists and terrorist organizations have been predominate in the convictions and cases pending since 2001: the physical movement of cash and the movement of funds through the banking system.[217] Funds moved through the banking system were placed into the banking system by directly depositing cash at a bank; giving cash to an individual or business operating as an unlicensed money transmitter who then deposits the funds into the individual's or business's bank account; or using a licensed MSB (with the help of complicit agents) to deposit funds into the licensed MSB's bank account. The physical movement of cash accounted for 28 percent of these cases while movement directly through banks constituted 22 percent; movement through licensed MSBs 17 percent, and movement by individuals or entities acting as unlicensed money transmitters constituted 18 percent.[218]

Further analysis of these cases suggests that, since 2007, defendants seeking to support terrorists and/or terrorist groups have tended to prefer licensed MSBs and unlicensed money transmitters as a point of entry into the banking system over banks. More than 30 percent of the identified funds transfers in TF cases prior to 2007 involved movement directly through banks, but this share drops to 8 percent for cases in and after 2007. Concurrently, the share of funds transfers identified in TF cases by licensed MSBs increased substantially, from approximately 5 percent to 30 percent. Additionally, physically moving cash (cash smuggling) to transfer funds from the United States increased from 22 percent to 37 percent, suggesting a desire to avoid transactions executed through financial institutions entirely. Financial institution reporting also indicates that certain Sunni extremist groups, such as certain AQ affiliates and Al-Shabaab, tend to use MSBs, while other terrorist groups, such as Hamas and Hizballah, appear to favor banks as a means of transmitting funds.[219]

1. *BANKS*

Banks are an attractive means for terrorist groups seeking to move funds globally because of the speed and ease at which they can move funds within the international financial system.[220] Through their global networks and inter-bank relationships, U.S. banks can instantly transfer funds for their customers almost anywhere in the world. Additionally, because of the importance of the United States to global financial markets activity, many foreign banks have established subsidiary branches or agencies in the United States to gain access to U.S.-based customers and to serve their own local customers' needs in the United States.

---

[217] *See* Footnote 89.

[218] The remaining 15 percent were a mix of checks, wire transfers through unspecified financial institutions, and TBML. *See* Footnote 89.

[219] Information derived from an analysis of financial institution BSA reporting. Additionally, funds related to Hamas and Hizballah account for approximately 40 percent of the funds blocked in U.S. financial institutions pursuant to E.O.s 12947 and 13224 and 18 U.S.C. § 2339B(a)(2) for affiliation with a SDGT, FTO or SDT. *See* OFAC, *2014 Terrorist Assets Report*.

[220] *See* FATF, Terrorist Financing, p. 21, February 2008.

In light of this vulnerability, the U.S. government has implemented an AML/CFT regulatory framework that includes robust implementation of targeted financial sanctions, which has made it more difficult for terrorists and their support networks to access the U.S. financial system. This framework aids financial institutions in identifying and managing risk, provides valuable information to law enforcement, and creates the foundation of financial transparency required to apply targeted financial measures against the various national security threats that seek to operate within the U.S. financial system.[221]

OFAC administers and enforces a vigorous sanctions regime in collaboration with the regulatory, law enforcement, and intelligence communities. Violators of U.S. economic sanctions can be subject to a range of administrative, civil and criminal penalties. The federal banking agencies[222] conduct regular examinations of banks to ensure compliance with BSA/AML programs, including ensuring that such institutions have an effective BSA/AML and OFAC compliance program that: identifies higher-risk areas, provides for appropriate internal controls for screening and reporting, establishes independent testing for compliance, designates an employee or employees as responsible for OFAC compliance, and creates training programs for appropriate personnel.[223] The SEC and CFTC impose similar requirements on financial institutions they supervise.

The enactment of the USA PATRIOT Act following the September 11, 2001 terrorist attacks enhanced the efforts of the U.S. government to prevent the U.S. financial system from being used to facilitate TF. For example, under Section 311 of the USA PATRIOT Act, the Secretary of the Treasury is authorized to find a foreign jurisdiction, foreign financial institution, class of international transactions, or type of account to be of primary money laundering concern, and to subsequently impose any one or a combination of special measures that U.S. financial institutions must take to protect the U.S. financial system, including from risks associated with TF.[224] These special measures range from enhanced due diligence, recordkeeping, and reporting requirements, up to and including, prohibition against establishing or maintaining any correspondent account or payable through account for or on behalf of a foreign financial institution, if the account involves a jurisdiction, financial institution, class of transaction, or type of account that is of primary money laundering concern. Treasury, through FinCEN, has utilized Section 311 to alert the U.S. financial system to TF threats associated with several foreign jurisdictions and foreign financial institutions, including: the Islamic Republic of Iran; LCB; the Commercial Bank of Syria (CBS) (including its subsidiary Syrian Lebanese Commercial Bank); Halawi Exchange Co.; and Kassem Rmeiti & Co.[225] In finding that CBS was a financial institution of primary money laundering concern, FinCEN noted that "numerous transactions that may be indicative of terrorist financing and

---

[221] David Cohen, Under Secretary for Terrorism and Financial Intelligence, Department of the Treasury, Testimony before the Senate Committee on Homeland Security and Governmental Affairs Permanent Subcommittee on Investigations, "U.S. Vulnerabilities to Money Laundering, Drugs, and Terrorist Financing: HSBC Case History," July 17, 2012. Available at http://www.hsgac.senate.gov/download/?id=55d94bbb-cbee-4a35-89ca-5493a12d73dd.

[222] For the purposes of the National TF Risk Assessment, the relevant federal banking agencies are the FRB, the FDIC, NCUA and OCC.

[223] The Federal Financial Institutions Examination Council (FFIEC) BSA/AML Examination Manual includes specific portions on compliance with OFAC's targeted financial sanctions regime. *See* FFIEC BSA/AML Manual 2014, pp. 145-154.

[224] *See* 31 U.S.C. § 5318A.

[225] A list of Section 311 Special Measures taken by FinCEN is available at http://www.fincen.gov/statutes_regs/patriot/section311.html.

money laundering have been observed transiting CBS," including "several transactions through accounts at CBS that reference a reputed financier for Osama bin Laden."[226]

In addition to Section 311, Sections 314(a) and 319 of the USA PATRIOT Act strengthened the U.S. government's ability to take specific regulatory actions to advance law enforcement investigations against TF threats. Section 314(a) allows law enforcement authorities to share information with financial institutions regarding individuals, entities, and organizations engaged in or reasonably suspected of engaging in terrorist acts and to determine whether the target of an investigation maintains an account at a particular financial institution.[227] Section 319(a) enhances law enforcement's ability to pursue assets overseas, while Section 319(b) provides law enforcement with summons and subpoena authority with respect to foreign banks that have correspondent accounts in the United States.[228]

Punitive measures and, for egregious cases, financial penalties, have been applied to banks determined to be out of compliance. For example, in December 2012, HSBC, a UK-headquartered financial institution with a substantial U.S. presence, was ordered to pay a total of approximately $1.9 billion in civil money penalties and asset forfeitures for various violations of U.S. AML and economic sanctions laws and regulations.[229] Furthermore, in a July 2014 settlement with U.S. regulators and law enforcement, BNP Paribas, in addition to having to pay a total of approximately $8.9 billion in criminal penalties and asset forfeitures, was subjected to a one-year long suspension of certain U.S. dollar-clearing services through its New York branch and other affiliates for business lines on which the misconduct centered.[230] FinCEN has also imposed civil money penalties against U.S. branches of foreign banks for failing to implement adequate due diligence procedures and internal controls that effectively managed the risk arising from the provision of foreign correspondent accounts or dollar-clearing services to financial institutions located in jurisdictions deemed a high-risk for money laundering and TF.[231]

<u>Misuse of Foreign Correspondent Banking</u>

The regulatory and enforcement actions taken by the U.S. government and the subsequent substantial financial and organizational investments by U.S.-based financial institutions have improved AML/CFT compliance among financial institutions.[232] However, the international financial system is interconnected

---

[226] FinCEN, *Imposition of a Special Measure Against Commercial Bank of Syria, Including Its Subsidiary, Syrian Lebanese Commercial Bank, as a Financial Institution of Primary Money Laundering Concern*, Notice of Proposed Rulemaking, 69 Fed. Reg. 28098, 28100, May 18, 2004.

[227] *See* 31 U.S.C. § 5318.

[228] *See* 18 U.S.C. § 981(k); 31 U.S.C. § 5318(k)(3).

[229] *See* OCC EA 2012-261, AA-EC-2012-140, December 4, 2012 and FRB Docket Nos. 12-062-CMP-FB, 12-062-CMPHC,and 12-062-B-FB, 2-4, December 11, 2012; FinCEN, *In the Matter of HSBC Bank USA, N.A. Mclean, Virginia*, No. 2012-02, December 10, 2012; *see also* Senate Permanent Subcommittee on Investigations, U.S. Vulnerabilities to Money Laundering, Drugs, and Terrorist Financing: HSBC Case History, at 210, July 16, 2012.

[230] *See* Department of Justice, Press Release, "BNP Paribas Agrees to Plead Guilty and to Pay $8.9 Billion for Illegally Processing Financial Transactions for Countries Subject to U.S. Economic Sanctions," June 30, 2014.

[231] *See* FinCEN, *In the Matter of Doha Bank, New York Branch, New York, New York*, No. 2009-1, April 20 2009; FinCEN, *In the Matter of The Federal Branch of Arab Bank, PLC, New York, New York*, No. 2005-2, August 17, 2005.

[232] For example, in its deferred prosecution agreement with the DOJ, HSBC noted that it had increased AML compliance spending nine –fold and AML staffing ten-fold between 2009 and 2011. *See* HSBC Bank USA, N.A. and HSBC Holdings plc DPA, ¶ 5, December 11, 2012.

and foreign financial institutions maintain correspondent accounts at and receive services from U.S. financial institutions in order to access the U.S. financial system. These relationships allow financial institutions worldwide to facilitate cross border transactions in the currency of choice. They also enable financial institutions to conduct business and provide services to clients in foreign countries without the expense and burden of establishing a foreign presence. However, some correspondent banking relationships are inherently higher-risk, in large part due to the challenges of "intermediation," where multiple intermediary financial institutions may be involved in a single funds transfer transaction. The complexity and volume of transactions that flow through U.S. correspondent accounts, coupled with the varying (often limited) recordkeeping requirements of funds transfer systems in different countries, increase the likelihood that funds associated with illicit finance, including TF, may flow through these accounts and into the U.S. financial system. These relationships could potentially indirectly expose a U.S. financial institution to risk, including TF, if the foreign financial institution does not effectively implement AML/CFT controls.

To help mitigate against this risk, certain U.S. financial institutions are required to conduct due diligence on their foreign correspondents to ensure that the foreign correspondent's controls are adequate to manage the risk to the U.S. financial institution associated with this relationship.[233] These U.S. financial institutions are also required to conduct enhanced due diligence on certain higher risk foreign correspondents which requires (1) enhanced scrutiny, (2) determining whether the foreign correspondent maintains nested accounts for other foreign banks, and (3) the collection of beneficial owner information regarding foreign correspondents that are not publicly traded.[234] In addition to these requirements for foreign correspondents, U.S. financial institutions are also prohibited from maintaining correspondent accounts for foreign "shell banks" (*i.e.*, foreign banks with no physical presence in any country).[235]

Despite these requirements, there have been isolated and particularly egregious instances of U.S. banks not adequately managing potential TF risks posed by their relationships with foreign financial institutions. In one case, the U.S. subsidiary of a foreign parent bank was found to have failed to collect or maintain customer due diligence information on non-U.S. banking affiliates of the foreign parent bank for which it maintained correspondent accounts.[236] This resulted in transactions flowing to and from the United States without appropriate monitoring and alerts to identify movements of funds.[237] A significant number of non-U.S. financial institutions and their customers gained indirect access to the U.S. financial system without appropriate safeguards.[238] These customers included foreign banks that were publicly associated with terrorist organizations or terrorist financing.[239]

---

[233] *See* 31 C.F.R. § 1010.610(a); FFIEC BSA/AML Manual, pp. 177-80.
[234] *See* 31 C.F.R. § 1010.610(b).
[235] *See* 31 C.F.R. § 1010.630.
[236] *See* FinCEN, *In the Matter of HSBC Bank USA, N.A. Mclean, Virginia*, No. 2012-02, December 10, 2012.
[237] *Id.*
[238] *Id.*
[239] *See* Senate Permanent Subcommittee on Investigations, U.S. Vulnerabilities to Money Laundering, Drugs, and Terrorist Financing: HSBC Case History, at 225, 228, July 16, 2012.

Risk Summary

As noted above, U.S. financial institutions face residual TF risk when foreign correspondents are not subject to the same or similar regulatory guidelines as U.S. banks, or do not have in place acceptable AML/CFT processes or controls.[240] This may be especially true where a foreign financial institution, based on its particular risk profile, which may include geographic profile, business line, or customer base, does not implement effective customer due diligence practices, suspicious activity identification processes, and/or recordkeeping.

2. *LICENSED MSBs*

The MSB industry in the United States is extremely diverse, ranging from Fortune 500 companies with numerous outlets and agents worldwide to small, independent "mom and pop" convenience stores in communities with population concentrations that do not necessarily have access to traditional banking services or in areas where English is rarely spoken. In addition, many MSBs only offer money services as an ancillary component to their primary business, such as a convenience store that cashes checks or a hotel that provides currency exchange.

As noted above, recent criminal prosecutions demonstrate that some TF facilitators have gravitated towards using licensed MSBs to place and transfer funds through the banking system. This trend has been more pronounced among certain Sunni extremist groups, such as certain AQ affiliates and Al-Shabaab, which tend to use MSBs, while other terrorist groups, such as Hamas and Hizballah, appear to favor banks as a means of transmitting funds.[241] In one case, an individual raised funds for Al-Shabaab from within the Somali diaspora in Missouri and elsewhere and used a variety of licensed MSBs with offices in the United States to remit the money to Somalia for general support of Al-Shabaab fighters. The co-conspirator, who worked in Minneapolis for one of the MSBs involved, helped the individual avoid leaving a paper trail by structuring transactions into low dollar amounts and by using false identification information. The MSB worker and other conspirators used fictitious names and phone numbers to hide the nature of their transactions.[242]

There is often overlap between some of the fund-raising methods that present a residual TF risk for the U.S. financial system and the use of MSBs to transfer them. For example, several individuals raising money under the auspices of charitable giving have used MSBs to transfer the funds to the terrorist organizations. In one case, an individual wanting to use a charitable organization as cover to send money to the Taliban eventually sent approximately $2,000 to Lahore, Pakistan via two separate MSB locations.[243] In a separate case, four Somali immigrants were convicted on a variety of TF-related charges, including conspiracy to provide material support to Al-Shabaab and money laundering. In this case, a worker at a licensed MSB was the conduit for moving the funds.[244] He conspired with two taxi

---

[240] *Id.*

[241] Information derived from an analysis of financial institution BSA reporting.

[242] *United States v. Mohamud Abdi Yusuf, et al.*, Case No. 4:10-cr-00547-HEA (E.D. Mo. October 2010).

[243] *New York v. Humayoun Ghoulam Nabi and Ismail Alsarabbi*, Q13800646, Q13800647 (Complaint) (N.Y. Crim. Ct. October 2013.

[244] *See* FBI, Press Release, "San Diego Jury Convicts Four Somali Immigrants of Providing Support to Foreign Terrorists, February 22, 2013.

drivers and the imam at a mosque to raise thousands of dollars for Al-Shabaab and send it back to Somalia. The defendants claimed to be motivated by charity and were trying to raise money for humanitarian purposes in Somalia. Evidence presented at trial indicated that thousands of dollars were solicited and raised via the mosque and from other taxi drivers. The defendants transferred funds from San Diego to Somalia through a now-defunct MSB in San Diego, structuring the transfers and using false names to conceal the destination of the funds. The MSB and its owner were charged in 2009 by the SEC for engaging in fraudulent activities.[245] The FBI also obtained transaction records from the MSB documenting the money transfers discussed in the recorded conversations.[246]

While these cases demonstrate the risk of licensed MSBs in the U.S. financial system serving as a conduit for TF, the U.S. government has endeavored to mitigate this risk through regulation and enforcement. As detailed in the National ML Risk Assessment, all MSB principals,[247] except for the U.S. Postal Service, are required to register with FinCEN[248] and to establish a written AML program reasonably designed to prevent the MSB from being used to facilitate money laundering and TF.[249] Additionally, the BSA requires MSBs to file CTRs[250] and SARs,[251] and maintain certain records. With limited exceptions, MSBs are also subject to reporting, recordkeeping and customer identification. Finally, 48 states have established supervisory requirements for MSBs, often including the requirement that an MSB be licensed with the state in which it is incorporated or does business.[252] The U.S. government continues to explore additional guidance and action that can be taken to allow the important legitimate business conducted by MSBs to continue while disrupting illicit activity.

Along with comprehensive regulatory requirements, FinCEN and U.S. law enforcement authorities have also pursued civil and criminal penalties against MSBs and individual employees who are complicit in facilitating TF. As described above, U.S. authorities have successfully prosecuted several MSBs and their employees who facilitated TF for providing material support to terrorist organizations, along with violations of other criminal statutes.[253] In addition to criminal charges brought by DOJ, FinCEN has the authority under the BSA to pursue civil enforcement actions against both MSBs and individual employees

---

[245] See SEC v. Shidall Express Inc. and Mohamud Abdi Ahmed, Case No. 3:09-cv-02610-JM-POR (S.D. Cal. filed November 19, 2009).

[246] See United States v. Moalin, No. 3:10-CR-4246 (JTM) (S.D. Cal. 2013).

[247] Many MSBs, including the vast majority of money transmitters in the United States, provide their services through agent relationships. While agents are not presently required to register with FinCEN, they are themselves MSBs that are required to establish AML programs and comply with the other recordkeeping and reporting requirements.

[248] See 31 C.F.R. § 1022.380.

[249] See 31 C.F.R. § 1022.210.

[250] See 31 C.F.R. § 1010.311.

[251] See 31 C.F.R. § 1022.320. Check cashers are not covered by the SAR requirement. See 31 CFR 1022.320(a)(1).

[252] At the federal level, MSBs are required to register with FinCEN and are examined for compliance with BSA requirements, which FinCEN has delegated to the IRS SB/SE division. Additionally, under the Money Remittances Improvement Act of 2014, Pub. L. 113–156, FinCEN may rely on examinations of MSBs for BSA compliance conducted by State supervisory agencies. State supervisory requirements vary, but general include licensing, capital and ownership requirements, and compliance with consumer protection and AML statutes.

[253] See, e.g., United States v. Ali, No. 0:10-CR-187, at *2 (MJD/FLN) (D. Minn. 2012); Government Response to Defendant's Sentencing Memorandum; United States v. Yusuf, No. 4:10-CR-00547-HEA (E.D. Mo. 2012), Government's Unclassified Memorandum; United States v. Moalin, No. 3:10-CR-4246 (JTM) (S.D. Cal. 2012).

for violations of the BSA that may contribute to TF, including the failure to abide by BSA reporting requirements.[254]

In light of the important role that non-bank financial institutions play in promoting financial inclusion, the U.S. government has made a sustained effort to create international standards and a domestic regulatory framework that protect consumers, expand financial access, and curtail money transmitter abuse by criminal actors and terrorist financiers. Treasury has led inter-governmental efforts over the past 15 years, working with money transmitters, banks, U.S. and foreign financial regulators and multilateral organizations such as the FATF, to establish domestic and international standards for the regulation and supervision of money transmitters.[255] As a result of these efforts, record volumes of remittances are being transmitted through legitimate and transparent channels.

Risk Summary

Despite these efforts, residual TF risk does remain for MSBs, especially for funds being moved from the United States on behalf of AQ and its affiliates, Al-Shabaab and South Asia-based terrorist groups, including TTP. As described in several of the cases noted above, licensed MSBs may be misused by complicit employees who willingly facilitate TF in violation of applicable laws, regulations and the MSBs own AML/CFT policies and procedures. The current $3,000 recordkeeping threshold results in the processing of the typical $200-$400 remittance without verifying customer identification, and these low value transactions by occasional customers presents a manageable TF risk because MSBs are required to file SARs when there is suspicion of ML or TF.[256]

3. *UNLICENSED MONEY TRANSMITTERS*

As detailed in the National ML Risk Assessment, along with licensed MSBs, there are also individuals and entities operating illegally as unlicensed money transmitters in the U.S. SARs filed by banks citing potential unlicensed money transmission activity identified a variety of businesses, including grocery or convenience stores, gas stations and liquor stores, which operated as unlicensed money transmitters.

A review of publicly available information on U.S. law enforcement cases involving TF offenses and financial reporting indicates that unlicensed money transmitters continue to be used to transfer illicit proceeds. For example, Saifullah Anjum Ranjha, a Pakistani national residing in the United States and operator of an unlicensed money remitter business in the District of Columbia, pleaded guilty to conspiring to launder money and to concealing TF. A cooperating witness, acting at the direction of law enforcement, held himself out to Ranjha as providing financing to members of AQ and its affiliated

---

[254] *See, e.g.,* FinCEN, *In the Matter of Saleh H. Adam dba Adam Service, Dearborn, Michigan* No, 2014-02, February 7, 2014; FinCEN, *In the Matter of Mohamed Mohamed-Abas Sheikh, Ann Arbor, Michigan*, No. 2011-9, September 23, 2011.
[255] *See, e.g.,* Daniel L. Glaser, Treasury Notes Blog, *Treasury's Work to Support Money Transmitters*, October 8, 2014. Available at http://www.treasury.gov/connect/blog/Pages/Treasury%E2%80%99s-Work-to-Support-Money-Transmitters.aspx.
[256] However, in their internal AML/CFT policies and procedures, some MSBs require customer identification for transactions below $3,000. *See* FinCEN, *Financial Institutions Outreach Initiative: Report on Outreach to Money Services Businesses*, p. 19, July 2010.

organizations. Over the course of four years, the cooperating witness gave Ranjha and his associates a total of $2,208,000 to transfer abroad, explaining that the funds were the proceeds of, and related to, his involvement in international drug trafficking, international smuggling of counterfeit cigarettes and weapons. Ranjha conducted 21 transactions in amounts ranging from $13,000 to $300,000. Ranjha arranged with his associates for the equivalent amount of monies, minus commissions, to be delivered to the cooperating witness, his third party designee, or a specified bank account in Canada, England, Spain, Pakistan, Japan and Australia.[257]

In light of the use by TF facilitators of unlicensed money transmitters, U.S. regulatory and law enforcement authorities have aggressively targeted these actors for investigation and prosecutions, with a targeted focus on the most significant violators. Importantly, 18 U.S.C. § 1960 imposes criminal penalties for the act of engaging in unlicensed money transmission, giving law enforcement and prosecutors a powerful tool to sanction violators regardless of whether their activity is used to facilitate TF. This can be especially useful for curtailing unlicensed money transmitter activity where proving the connection to TF may be difficult or pose particular evidentiary challenges. As noted above in August 2011, Mohammad Younis pleaded guilty to a violation of 18 U.S.C. § 1960 for running an unlicensed money transmitter that transferred funds to many individuals, including Faisal Shahzad, who later used the funds for his attempt to detonate a car bomb in Times Square.[258] Because Section 1960 does not require proving a connection to TF, U.S. authorities were able to shut down a potential TF source without having to prove Younis knowingly facilitated the funds transfers for terrorist activity. In addition to prosecuting unlicensed money transmitters, the U.S. government has also worked with financial institutions to more effectively detect and report potential unlicensed money transmission. For example, FinCEN has issued detailed guidance to financial institutions on how to report suspicious activity associated with unregistered MSBs.[259]

Risk Summary

The ongoing challenge of identifying unlicensed money transmitters, which largely serve populations that cannot or choose not to use legitimate channels, raises the specter of illegal transactions that may support terrorist groups including AQ and its affiliates, Al-Shabaab and TTP, and poses a residual risk for TF.

4. *CASH SMUGGLING*

As robust implementation of AML/CFT controls across financial institutions has raised the costs, risks and difficulty for TF networks operating within the financial system, cash smuggling has become an increasingly attractive way for foreign terrorists to transfer funds. The use of cash is attractive to criminals mainly because of its anonymity, portability, liquidity and lack of audit trail.

---

[257] *See* Department of Justice, Press Release, "Money Remitter Pleads Guilty To Money Laundering Conspiracy And Concealing Terrorist Financing," August 22, 2008.

[258] *See* Department of Justice, Press Release, "Long Island Man Pleads Guilty in Manhattan Federal Court to Engaging in Hawala Activity that Funded Attempted Times Square Bombing," August 18, 2011.

[259] *See* FinCEN Advisory, *Informal Value Transfer Systems*, FIN-2010-A011, September, 1, 2010.

According to the surveyed cases, since 2007, 18 TF-related prosecutions in the United States have in some way involved the use of cash to transfer funds to terrorist organizations.[260] These cases have involved various FTOs, including core AQ, AQ in Iraq (the predecessor organization to ISIL), AQAP, Al-Shabaab, Hizballah, and FARC. There have been several notable cases in which U.S.-based individuals sought to smuggle cash for the benefit of Hizballah by concealing it in vehicles. On May 21, 2012, an individual was sentenced to more than six years in prison for conspiring to send hundreds of thousands of dollars to Hizballah.[261] His wife and co-conspirator previously pleaded guilty to one count of conspiracy to provide material support and resources to a FTO. During multiple meetings with an FBI confidential source, the two defendants discussed ways to secretly send money to Hizballah leaders in Lebanon.[262] The two defendants proposed several methods, including using wealthy individuals with property in Lebanon to act as unlicensed money transmittal services and by using legitimate U.S. businesses that deal primarily in cash to over-report revenue, which would be taxed and therefore "legitimately" declared during transport to Lebanon.[263] The two defendants also proposed sending funds through couriers, who would carry cash in amounts less than the $10,000 reporting requirement either directly to Lebanon, where it would be recovered by co-conspirators and delivered to Hizballah, or to a third country, where it would be transferred to an offshore account and wire transferred to co-conspirators in Lebanon.[264] Alternatively, money orders in amounts less than the $3,000 record-keeping requirement could be sent to post office boxes in a third country where they would be deposited in an offshore account and transferred by wire to Lebanon.[265] One of the defendants indicated that he had previously carried about $66,000 on his person over the course of two trips to Lebanon.[266] He also indicated that he understood the funds would be sent to a designated terrorist organization and used to target Israel. The fact that the two defendants, after discussing multiple options to transfer the funds, ultimately agreed to send approximately $500,000 by concealing it inside a car, which they planned to send to Lebanon via a container ship, demonstrates how terrorist supporters were compelled to resort to cash smuggling – a less efficient means of funds transfer – in an effort to avoid U.S. controls.[267]

Similarly, on July 31, 2012, a Virginia resident pled guilty to attempted money laundering for placing what he believed to be $100,000 belonging to Hizballah inside a Jeep in 2010 and directing it to be shipped to Beirut; his arrest was the result of an FBI-orchestrated sting operation.[268] In a similar case, two Iraqi nationals pleaded guilty to TF-related charges resulting from an FBI-led sting operation.[269] From September 2010 through May 2011, one Iraqi participated in ten separate operations to send weapons and money that he believed was destined for terrorists in Iraq. In January 2011, he recruited the

---

[260] *See* Footnote 89.

[261] FBI, Press Release, "Ohio Man Sentenced to 75 Months in Prison for Scheme to Send Money to Hizballah," May 21, 2012. Available at http://www.fbi.gov/cleveland/press-releases/2012/ohio-man-sentenced-to-75-months-in-prison-for-scheme-to-send-money-to-hizballah.

[262] *See United States v. Hor and Amera Akl*, No. 3:10-cr-00251-JGC, (N.D. Ohio, filed June 7, 2010).

[263] *Id.*

[264] *Id.*

[265] *Id.*

[266] *See United States v. Hor and Amera Akl*, No. 3:10-cr-00251-JGC (Indictment) (N.D. Ohio, filed June 7, 2010) .

[267] *Id.*

[268] *See United States v. Mufid Kamal Mrad*, Case No. 1:12mj363 (Affidavit) (E.D. Va. May 30, 2012); *see also* FBI, Press Release, "Vienna Man Pleads Guilty to Attempted Money Laundering," July 31, 2012.

[269] *United States v. Alwan et al*, Case No. 1:11-cr-00013 (Indictment) (W.D. Ky. 2011); Department of Justice, Press Release, "Iraqi National Pleads Guilty to 12-count Terrorism Indictment in Kentucky," August 21, 2012.

second defendant to assist in these material support operations. Over the course of the conspiracy, the individual believed he had sent $375,000 cash alone and $565,000 cash with the help of the second defendant. The primary means of smuggling the cash was in a hidden compartment of a tractor-trailer which would then be sent on to Iraq.[270]

These case studies demonstrate that cash couriers are being used to transfer funds to terrorist organizations. The U.S. government, particularly LEAs, proactively investigates and prosecutes such cases of abuse in order to effectively mitigate the vulnerability. For example, DHS, through ICE and CBP, has established special programs and initiatives to target bulk cash smuggling across U.S. borders.[271] DOJ and other prosecutorial authorities have levied criminal penalties for failing to report the cross-border transfer of currency in excess of $10,000.[272] Additionally, as detailed in the National ML Risk Assessment, the misuse of cash is limited by transaction recordkeeping and reporting requirements that require financial institutions to verify a customer's identity and retain records of certain information prior to issuing or selling payment instruments when purchased with currency in amounts between $3,000 and $10,000.[273] For cash transactions above $10,000, whether a single transaction or a series of related transactions with a customer in a single business day, financial institutions are required to file a CTR with FinCEN.[274] Other non-financial businesses must report cash transactions of more than $10,000 to the IRS and FinCEN.[275]

Risk Summary

It is difficult – if not impossible – to completely stop the use of cash smuggling, and thus, it remains a residual TF risk. Combined with the widespread demand for U.S. currency globally, multiple terrorist groups, including AQ and its affiliates, ISIL, Al-Shabaab, Hizballah, and FARC, will continue to use cash smuggling as a less efficient alternative for moving funds globally.

C. POTENTIAL EMERGING TF THREATS AND VULNERABILITIES

1. CYBERCRIME AND IDENTITY THEFT

In addition to the various methods of raising funds described above, U.S. authorities are closely monitoring TF activity to identify potential new strategies of fundraising that may be employed by terrorist organizations. For example, a variety of terrorist organizations, including AQ and Hizballah, could use successful cybercrime schemes employed by criminal actors to directly steal funds, or alternatively, steal information or other assets that could then be sold in online black markets.[276] Terrorist

---

[270] Id.

[271] See Department of Homeland Security, Disrupt Terrorist Financing. Available at http://www.dhs.gov/topic/disrupt-terrorist-financing.

[272] See 31 U.S.C. § 5332.

[273] See 31 C.F.R. § 1010.415.

[274] See 31 U.S.C. § 5313.

[275] See 31 U.S.C. § 5331 and 26 U.S.C. § 6050I.

[276] See, Gordon M. Snow, Assistant Director, FBI Cyber Division, Statement Before the Senate Judiciary Committee, Subcommittee on Crime and Terrorism, April 12, 2011. Available at http://www.fbi.gov/news/testimony/cybersecurity-responding-to-the-threat-of-cyber-crime-and-terrorism.

organizations may also use various identity theft schemes to raise funds, particularly given the substantial revenues that can be generated from these schemes.[277] While terrorist groups have stolen credit cards to raise funds in the past, as well as to evade detection by law enforcement, the proliferation of stolen identities and their sale in various online forums make them an attractive fundraising scheme.[278]

2. *ISIL*

U.S. authorities are also actively monitoring attempts by ISIL to raise funds from U.S. persons and move funds through U.S. financial institutions. While ISIL receives the vast majority of its revenue from criminal and terrorist activities in Syria and Iraq, including the exploitation of local resources, extortion of the local population and KFR, coalition efforts to disrupt these sources of funding may force ISIL to look elsewhere for new revenue, including increasing fundraising from individuals in the United States.[279] U.S. law enforcement authorities have identified isolated cases of U.S. persons who have provided or attempted to provide funds to ISIL, as well as U.S. persons who have traveled or attempted to travel overseas to serve as foreign terrorist fighters with or otherwise support ISIL.[280] Additionally, ISIL may also seek to exploit Iraqi and Syrian bank branches or other financial institutions that it controls to conduct international transactions, which would allow it to more easily receive foreign funds to finance its activities as well as send payments abroad to procure weapons and other goods to sustain itself. U.S. authorities, working with international partners, are taking measures to prevent ISIL from accessing the international financial system, including U.S. financial institutions.[281]

3. *NEW PAYMENT SYSTEMS*

As detailed in the National ML Risk Assessment, virtual currencies such as Bitcoin and other emerging payments technologies, while representing an opportunity for financial innovation, have attracted the attention of various criminal groups, and may be vulnerable to abuse by terrorist financiers. For example, the U.S. Secret Service has observed that criminals are looking for and finding virtual currencies that offer anonymity for both users and transactions; the ability to move illicit proceeds from one country to another quickly; low volatility, which results in lower exchange risk; widespread adoption in the criminal underground; and trustworthiness.[282] In terms of TF risk, there has been some speculation about using

---

[277] DOJ estimated direct and indirect losses from identity theft at approximately $24.7 billion in 2012. *See* Erika Harrell, Ph.D. and Lynn Langton, Ph.D., DOJ, Office of Justice Programs, Bureau of Justice Statistic, Victims of Identity Theft, 2012. Available at http://www.bjs.gov/content/pub/pdf/vit12.pdf.

[278] *See* FATF, Terrorist Financing, p.17, February 2008.

[279] Jennifer Fowler, Deputy Assistant Secretary for Terrorist Financing and Financial Crimes, Remarks at the Washington Institute for Near East Policy on U.S. Efforts to Counter the Financing of ISIL, February 2, 2015. Available at http://www.treasury.gov/press-center/press-releases/Pages/jl9755.aspx.

[280] *See, e.g.,* Department of Justice, Press Release, "Six Defendants Charged with Conspiracy and Providing Material Support to Terrorists," February 6, 2015. In addition, in October 2014, U.S. authorities detained three teenage girls who flew from Colorado to Germany in an attempt to travel on to Syria and join the Islamic State.

[281] Jennifer Fowler, Deputy Assistant Secretary for Terrorist Financing and Financial Crimes, Remarks at the Washington Institute for Near East Policy on U.S. Efforts to Counter the Financing of ISIL, February 2, 2015.

[282] Edward Lowery III , USSS Criminal Investigative Division Special Agent in Charge Testimony Before the U.S. Senate Committee on Homeland Security and Governmental Affairs hearing titled "Beyond Silk Road: Potential Risks, Threats, and Promises of Virtual Currencies," November 18, 2013.

virtual currency to transfer funds overseas. For example, a posting on a blog linked to ISIL has proposed using Bitcoin to fund global jihadist efforts.[283]

In light of this risk, U.S. law enforcement authorities have aggressively investigated and prosecuted individuals and entities that have attempted to use virtual currencies for illicit activities. Liberty Reserve, for example, a virtual currency based in Costa Rica, its principal founder, and six others were charged in federal court in New York in 2013 with money laundering and illegally operating as an unlicensed money transmitter.[284] The defendants were convicted in 2013 and 2014. Before founding Liberty Reserve, the business's principal had been convicted in the United States for operating "Gold Age," an E-Gold exchanger. The Secret Service estimates that Liberty Reserve had more than one million users worldwide, with more than 200,000 in the United States, and processed more than $1.4 billion of transactions annually.[285] The transactions processed through Liberty Reserve involved payments associated with credit card fraud, identity theft, investment fraud, computer hacking, drug trafficking, and child pornography.[286]

With an eye to both stopping financial crime and permitting socially beneficial financial innovation to occur, U.S. regulators have sought to develop a coherent framework for regulating emerging payment systems and virtual currencies.[287] Given the attractiveness of virtual currency to conduct illicit financial transactions, the possibility exists that terrorist groups may use these new payment systems to transfer funds collected in the United States to terrorist groups and their supporters located outside of the United States, although the degree to which this presents a residual TF risk is unclear.

---

[283] *See* Coindesk, "ISIS-Linked Blog: Bitcoin Can Fund Terrorist Movements Worldwide," July 17, 2014. Available at http://www.coindesk.com/isis-bitcoin-donations-fund-jihadist-movements/.

[284] *See United States v. Liberty Reserve, S.A., et al.*, 13 Crim. 368 (S.D.N.Y. May 20, 2013).

[285] Edward Lowery III , USSS Criminal Investigative Division Special Agent in Charge Testimony Before the U.S. Senate Committee on Homeland Security and Governmental Affairs hearing titled "Beyond Silk Road: Potential Risks, Threats, and Promises of Virtual Currencies", November 18, 2013.

[286] Jennifer Shaskey Calvery, Director, FinCEN, Department of the Treasury, Testimony Before the U.S. Senate Committee on Homeland Security and Government Affairs hearing titled "Beyond Silk Road: Potential Risks, Threats, and Promises of Virtual Currencies," November 18, 2013.

[287] *See, e.g.,* FinCEN FIN-2013-G001, Application of FinCEN's Regulations to Persons Administering, Exchanging, or Using Virtual Currencies, March 18, 2013; New York Department of Financial Services, Press Release, "NY DFS Releases Proposed BitLicense Regulatory Framework for Virtual Currency Firms," July 17, 2014.

CONCLUSION

CONCLUSION

To combat the threat posed by TF, the U.S. government has developed and implemented a comprehensive interagency approach to aggressively investigate and prosecute all forms of TF occurring in the United States, close existing gaps in the U.S. financial system that have been used to facilitate TF, designate financiers for economic sanctions to isolate them from the global financial system, and engage international partners and institutions to develop a secure global framework that will effectively prevent TF from infiltrating the global financial system.

Although this effort has been effective in reducing the overall vulnerability of the United States and U.S. financial system to TF, certain residual risks still remain. Terrorists and terrorist organizations continue to engage in criminal activity in the United States, including benefitting from drug trafficking, to raise funds. To combat this, the U.S. government uses sophisticated interagency information-sharing, investigations, designations and prosecutions, aided by powerful legal authorities and tools, to target such criminal activity.

Although the charitable sector continues to face vulnerability to abuse by TF facilitators, a coordinated law enforcement, regulatory and outreach effort by the U.S. government, working within government and with charitable organizations, has improved the resiliency of the charitable sector to such abuse and forced potential TF fundraisers to pursue fundraising activity outside of charitable organizations. A notable trend in this sector has seen individuals unaffiliated with any charitable organization recognized by the U.S. government raise funds for terrorist organizations under the auspices of charity, with outreach through social media playing a key role. In response, the U.S. government has deployed interagency and joint resources to identify, investigate and prosecute these facilitators.

Finally, individuals based in the United States have also given funds directly to terrorist groups, or raised funds for their own terrorist activities, including funding travel to join militant groups overseas. While these types of transactions are particularly difficult to detect, law enforcement and the regulatory community continue to develop new tools to identify, investigate and prosecute these individuals.

Given the central role U.S. banks play in facilitating global payments, the United States is vulnerable to the movement of funds associated with TF through the banking system. To address this, the U.S. government has focused on developing and implementing preventive measures to reduce the vulnerability of these institutions to TF, used additional tools and authorities to more effectively target TF, and imposed substantial financial penalties on noncompliant institutions. Even with these measures, the U.S. banking system is exposed to residual TF risk, such as from foreign correspondents that may not have effective AML/CFT programs.

Although TF facilitators may seek to abuse MSBs to move funds through the banking system, financial regulatory and outreach efforts have mitigated much of the potential vulnerability, although residual risk remains, especially from complicit MSB employees assisting TF facilitators. The U.S. government has also aggressively prosecuted persons or entities operating as unlicensed money transmitters and worked with financial institutions to develop measures to more effectively recognize such activity; however, given the difficulty in identifying these transactions and their observed use to facilitate TF, some residual risk does remain. Finally, as AML/CFT measures, prosecutions and outreach have forced terrorist groups out of the regulated financial system, they have increasingly favored less efficient means of moving funds, such as cash smuggling.

In addition to the residual risks identified, the U.S. government continues to monitor and review potential emerging TF threats and vulnerabilities, including the use of new payment technologies and growing links between online criminal activity and TF. To identify and combat these emerging threats and vulnerabilities, the U.S. law enforcement, intelligence and regulatory communities will continue to collaborate and share information, utilize legal authorities and tools to sanction and prosecute TF facilitators, and reach out to private sector and international partners to improve the understanding of such threats. As a leader in the global economy and international financial system, the United States is committed to continuing to develop and implement effective CFT measures to further reduce TF risks in the United States and to the U.S. financial system.